KEY FACTS

EVIDENCE

GW00399937

3rd edition

Emma Washbourne

HODDER
EDUCATION
AN HACHETTE UK COMPANY

Orders: please contact Bookpoint Ltd, 130 Milton Park, Abingdon, Oxon OX14 4SB.
Telephone: (44) 01235 827720. Fax: (44) 01235 400454. Lines are open from 9.00–5.00, Monday
to Saturday, with a 24-hour message answering service. You can also order through
our website www.hoddereducation.co.uk

British Library Cataloguing in Publication Data
A catalogue record for this title is available from The British Library.

ISBN 978 1 444 11 862 9

First published 2003
Second Edition 2006
This Edition 2010
Impression number   10 9 8 7 6 5 4 3 2 1
Year   2010   2011   2012

Hachette UK's policy is to use papers that are natural, renewable and recyclable products and
made from wood grown in sustainable forests. The logging and manufacturing processes are
expected to conform to the environmental regulations of the country of origin.

Typeset by Transet Limited, Coventry, Warwickshire.
Printed in Great Britain for Hodder Education, an Hachette UK company, 338 Euston Road,
London NW1 3BH by Cox & Wyman Limited, Reading, Berkshire.

Contents

List of cases

Preface

Every course in Evidence involves an examination of a myriad of rules and exceptions, set against a backdrop of judicial discretion to exclude evidence. Those rules, though separately considered, fit together like a jigsaw to establish an overall picture. In order to achieve an understanding of the subject, it is necessary, having considered each rule in isolation, to focus on the wider picture. A prudent student will not rely upon question spotting; what is required is a sound understanding and competence in applying all the rules and exceptions, because in a trial situation, and indeed on an examination paper, each and every rule is potentially applicable. This book aims to help students see the wider picture. It serves as a reminder of the essential technicalities of the subject. The format, which utilises lists, bullet points and diagrams, should ease the difficulties of memorising the rules and the relevant cases.

The third edition includes details of up-to-date cases, across the rules covered by the book, but particularly in the areas of character and convictions and hearsay evidence. It also incorporates provisions relating to witness anonymity introduced by the Coroners and Justice Act 2009; the extension of special measures to vulnerable defendants through the Police and Justice Act 2006 and references to the new Criminal Procedure Rules which came into force on 5th April 2010.

At the time of writing, key changes to the availability of special measures made by the Coroners and Justice Act 2009 are not yet in force, but students should monitor developments in this area. An important decision of the Grand Chamber of the European Court of Human Rights in the case of *Al-Khawaja v United Kingdom*, relating to the admissibility of 'sole and decisive' hearsay evidence, is also awaited. Again, students should follow developments in this area.

1

An introduction to the Law of Evidence

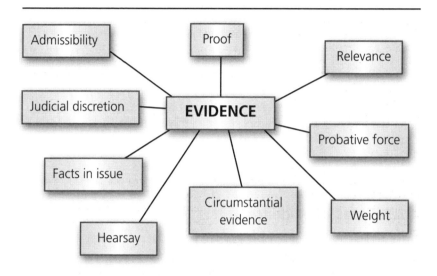

1.1 Introduction

This introductory chapter deals with the preliminaries: important definitions, the distinction between relevance and admissibility and the nature of judicial discretion. Finally it focuses briefly on human rights, identifying those rules of evidence which are most likely to be affected by the Human Rights Act (HRA) 1998.

1.2 The function of judge and jury

1. In a criminal trial at Crown Court, judges are responsible for deciding matters of law and ensuring that trials are conducted fairly.

2. Judges have discretion to exclude admissible evidence

(a) at common law (because its prejudicial effect outweighs its probative value) and

(b) under s78(1) Police and Criminal Evidence Act (PACE) 1984 where its admission would have 'such an adverse effect on the fairness of the proceedings that the court ought not to admit it'.

3. The judge is obliged to sum up the case to the jury at the conclusion of the evidence, reminding them of the facts and directing them on the law.

4. The jury's responsibility is to decide questions of fact. The assessment of weight, the probative force of evidence, and the credibility of witnesses are matters for the jury.

5. In a civil trial the judge assumes responsibility for deciding questions of law and fact. In the absence of a jury, there is no requirement for the judge to sum up the facts or to offer directions on the law.

1.3 Definitions and concepts

1.3.1 Types of evidence

In a criminal trial, evidence is the means by which the prosecution tries to prove its case and the defendant tries to cast doubt upon the prosecution's evidence. Similarly in a civil case, it is through adducing evidence that the claimant attempts to prove his case and the defendant attempts to counter the claimant's case.

1. **Oral evidence or 'testimony'** is the most common form of evidence: a witness tells the court in his own words what he has seen or heard. He will then be cross-examined in order that the testimony can be assessed. Evidence given by television/video link is also classed as oral evidence.

2. **Documentary evidence** is admissible in certain circumstances, although oral testimony is generally preferred. Documentary evidence includes films, tapes, video recordings, etc. Documentary evidence is a form of 'real evidence'.

3. **Real evidence** is normally something tangible that is produced for inspection by the court, such as the murder weapon; an intangible form of real evidence would be a viewing of the scene of an incident by the tribunal of fact.

4. **Direct or 'percipient' evidence** is testimony that relates to the direct perception of a fact in issue, for example 'I saw him stab her with a pair of scissors'.

5. **Circumstantial evidence** is evidence from which an inference needs to be drawn by the tribunal of fact before a fact in issue is proved. Circumstantial evidence requires the tribunal of fact to decide
   (i) whether the relevant facts, or some of them, are proved, and if so
   (ii) whether the fact in issue should be inferred from the existence of those facts.
   An example of circumstantial evidence would be: 'I saw the accused running from the area where the body of the deceased was found. He was holding a blood-stained knife'. The jury would need to decide firstly whether they believed that evidence; and secondly whether they could infer from that evidence that the accused had killed the deceased.

6. **Primary evidence** is the best evidence there can be of a fact, for example the original contract as opposed to a photocopy.

7. **Secondary evidence** indicates that better evidence exists, so the photocopied contract would be secondary evidence.

8. **Insufficient evidence** is evidence that is so weak that no reasonable person could decide an issue in reliance upon that evidence alone.

9. *Prima facie* evidence is sufficient to prove a fact in the absence of any contradictory evidence.

10. A *voir dire* may also be referred to as a 'trial within a trial'. This is a procedure used to determine, for example, the competence of a witness to testify, or the admissibility of a disputed confession. In trials on indictment, a *voir dire* is normally held in the absence of the jury.

1.3.2 Admissibility, relevance and weight of evidence

1. Evidence is admissible if it is receivable by the court. It is a precondition for admissibility that evidence is **relevant** (*R v Turner* (1975)). A court may reject evidence because it is irrelevant, or insufficiently relevant to the facts in issue. *In R v Randall* (2004) Lord Steyn explained: 'A judge ruling on a point of admissibility involving an issue of relevance has to decide whether the evidence is capable of

increasing or diminishing the probability of the existence of a fact in issue. The question of relevance is typically a matter of degree to be determined, for the most part, by common sense and experience'.

2. Relevant evidence is that which makes the fact requiring proof more or less probable. It was defined by Lord Simon of Glaisdale in *DPP v Kilbourne* (1973) in the following terms: 'Evidence is relevant if it is logically probative or disprobative of some matter which requires proof'.

3. Only three types of evidence are admissible:

   (i) Facts in issue

   (a) In a criminal case, the facts in issue are those facts that the prosecution must prove in order to establish the guilt of the defendant, together with those facts raised by way of defence that the prosecution must normally disprove.

   (b) In a civil case, the facts in issue are those facts that the claimant must prove in order to establish his case, together with those facts that the defendant must prove to establish a defence, for example contributory negligence or *volenti*.

   (c) What facts are in issue in any case will therefore depend upon the substantive law that is applicable and any defence that is raised.

   (ii) Facts relevant to a fact in issue: otherwise known as **circumstantial evidence**.

   (a) This is evidence from which an inference needs to be drawn by the tribunal of fact (judge, jury or bench of magistrates, depending upon the nature and mode of trial) before a fact in issue is proved.

   (b) A fact is relevant to a fact in issue if its existence makes proof or disproof of a fact in issue more likely.

   (iii) Collateral facts relate to a witness rather than directly to the facts in issue; an eyewitness may, for example, be asked questions to establish whether he has good or poor vision.
   Note: Any evidence which does not fall into one of the above three categories is **irrelevant** and **inadmissible**.

4. Even where evidence is relevant, it may be excluded if it falls foul of any of the exclusionary rules of the English law of evidence. These rules have evolved to protect defendants and ensure a fair trial.

5. Once it has been decided that evidence is relevant and admissible, the jury will need to decide what 'weight' to attach to it. 'Weight' refers

to the probative value or strength evidence has in relation to the facts in issue. The jury will make a subjective assessment of the evidence, considering factors such as truthfulness of the witness and reliability of the evidence.

1.4 Judicial discretion

1. Under many of the 'rules', judges are given the responsibility of making judgements, for example weighing the probative value of evidence against its prejudicial effect.

2. Under s78(1) PACE 1984, judges have a statutory duty to ensure the fairness of criminal trials by excluding: 'any evidence on which the prosecution proposes to rely ... if it appears to the court that, having regard to all the circumstances, including the circumstances in which the evidence was obtained, the admission of the evidence would have such an adverse effect on the fairness of the proceedings that the court ought not to admit it'.

3. The s78(1) discretion may be used to exclude an otherwise admissible confession, identification evidence or any other prosecution evidence in the interests of fairness.

4. There is no corresponding 'inclusionary' discretion to include inadmissible evidence in the interests of fairness except under s114(1)(d) Criminal Justice Act (CJA) 2003, where hearsay evidence may be admitted in the interests of justice (see 9.3).

5. Neither is there a general discretion to exclude relevant evidence adduced by the defence on the grounds of fairness.

1.5 The Human Rights Act 1998

The HRA 1998 has paved the way for a number of challenges involving rules of evidence. The most obvious areas relate to:

1. reverse burdens of proof (where legislation imposes a legal burden of proof on a defendant in relation to a specific defence (see 2.5);

2. the exercise of judicial discretion to exclude under s78 PACE 1984 (see 11.3);

3. the prohibition upon defendants cross-examining complainants in sexual cases on previous sexual acts under s41 of the Youth Justice and Criminal Evidence Act 1999 (see 4.5);

4. The admission of hearsay evidence from an absent witness under s116(1) CJA 2003.

1.5.1 Article 6

The potential impact of the HRA 1998 is assessed at various stages throughout this book. The most relevant of the rights protected by the HRA 1998 are under Article 6, the right to a fair trial. Article 6(1) covers trials 'determining civil rights and obligations' as well as criminal charges. Article 6 guarantees:

    (a) a fair and public hearing within a reasonable time by an independent and impartial tribunal;

    (b) the presumption of innocence until guilt is established;

    (c) certain minimum rights including:

        (i) the right to be informed of the nature of the charge;

        (ii) adequate time and facilities to prepare a defence;

        (iii) the right to legal assistance;

        (iv) the right to examine opposing witnesses;

        (v) the assistance of an interpreter where necessary.

Note: The case of *Neumeister v Austria* (1979–80) developed the concept of equality of arms. 'Each party must be afforded a reasonable opportunity to present his case … under conditions that do not place him at a substantial disadvantage *vis-à-vis* his opponent'. This principle has particular relevance to prosecution disclosure requirements (see 13.8.1).

1.6 The Criminal Procedure Rules 2010

Procedural matters in criminal trials are now governed by the Criminal Procedure Rules 2010, which came into force on 5th April 2010, consolidating The Criminal Procedure Rules 2005 and amendments made to them via various statutory instruments. The approach is similar to that adopted in civil proceedings under the Civil Procedure Rules 1998. The Criminal Procedure Rules are available online from www.justice.gov.uk and the most relevant parts for students of Evidence are:

Part 1 — The overriding objective
Part 22 — Disclosure
Part 29 —Measures to assist a witness or defendant to give evidence
Part 33 — Expert evidence
Part 34 — Hearsay evidence
Part 35 — Evidence of bad character
Part 36 — Evidence of a complainant's previous sexual behaviour.

2

The burdens and standards of proof

2.1 The burden of proof in criminal cases

The legal and evidential burdens at various stages of a criminal trial

PROSECUTION CASE

DEFENCE CASE

The legal burden is on the prosecution throughout the case to prove every element of the offence charged.

Defendant MAY have a legal burden in relation to a specific defence raised. The legal burden does not shift from prosecution to defence.

The evidential burden is on the prosecution to produce evidence on every element of the offence charged sufficient to 'pass the judge'.

Once the prosecution has successfully passed the judge then the evidential burden passes to the defendant.

BUT

The burden is less onerous than that which lies with the prosecution: if the defendant fails to produce evidence he will not necessarily lose the case.

Once a proper foundation for a defence has been laid by the defendant, the prosecution has the legal burden of disproving that defence.

Where the defendant raises a defence that goes beyond a denial of the prosecution case then he must lay a proper foundation for that defence.

2.2 Definitions

- The **legal** burden is the burden to prove or disprove a fact in issue;
- The **evidential** burden is merely a burden to produce evidence.

2.3 The legal burden in criminal cases: general rule

1. In criminal proceedings the prosecution bears the legal burden of proving every element of the offence charged, and disproving any defences raised, beyond reasonable doubt (*Woolmington v DPP* (1935));

2. The legal burden never shifts except where presumptions operate (see 2.4.6);

3. Whether or not the legal burden has been discharged is decided at the conclusion of the evidence by the tribunal of fact (jury or bench of magistrates).

2.3.1 The legal burden in criminal cases: exceptions to the general rule

A legal burden may be placed on an accused in relation to a specific defence raised. This is a new legal burden requiring the defendant to prove the defence on a balance of probabilities. Examples of 'reverse burdens' by virtue of a defence raised include:

1. **Common law:** Insanity under the M'Naughten rules;
2. **Express statutory exceptions** include:
    - Section 2 Homicide Act 1957: where diminished responsibility is raised as a defence to a charge of murder (*R v Dunbar* (1958));
    - Section 1(1) Prevention of Crime Act 1953: where the accused relies on a defence of lawful authority or reasonable excuse in response to a charge of possession of an offensive weapon;
    - Section 2 Prevention of Corruption Act 1916: where a gift is given or received by a public official, it will be presumed that the gift was given or received corruptly unless the contrary is proved by the accused.
    - These exceptions are illustrative examples only: research suggests that up to 40% of offences tried in Crown Court impose a legal burden on the accused.

3. **Implied statutory exceptions** by virtue of s101 Magistrates' Court Act 1981 which states: 'Where the defendant … relies for his defence on any exception, exemption, proviso, excuse or qualification, the burden of proving that he falls within that exception, proviso, excuse or qualification shall be on him'.

   ■ The importance of s101 is that it places a legal burden on the defendant where he relies upon a defence provided by statute to a limited class of people, for example, licence holders.

   ■ The scope of the exception was widened by *R v Edwards* (1975) where it was held that s101 Magistrates' Court Act 1981 is merely 'declaratory of the English law' and applies both to summary trials and trials on indictment.

   ■ The House of Lords in *R v Hunt* (1987) offered guidelines to courts charged with construing statutes in accordance with s101:

      (i) It should not easily be inferred that Parliament intended to impose a legal burden on the accused;

      (ii) Courts should have regard to the intention of Parliament and the mischief at which the section is aimed;

      (iii) Courts should have regard to the ease or difficulty a party would have in discharging the legal burden (see *R v Clarke (Roy)* (2008));

      (iv) The more serious the offence, the less likely that Parliament would have intended to impose a legal burden on the accused;

      (v) Where the statute is ambiguous, the accused should be given the benefit of the doubt (see *DPP v Wright* (2009)).

2.4 The evidential burden in criminal cases

■ Where a party has only an evidential burden on an issue, there is no obligation upon him to prove that issue; he is merely expected or required to adduce evidence.

■ The nature of the evidential burden in a criminal case changes during the course of a trial.

Students should understand the nature of the evidential burden in the following situations:

1. where the evidential burden is borne by the prosecution at the start of the trial (see 2.4.1);

2. where the evidential burden is borne by the accused at the close of the prosecution case (see 2.4.2);

3. where the evidential burden is borne by the accused by virtue of a defence which goes beyond a denial of the prosecution case (see 2.4.3);

4. where the evidential burden is borne by the accused by virtue of his reliance upon the defence of non-insane automatism (see 2.4.4).

2.4.1 The evidential burden on the prosecution at the start of the trial

1. At the start of a trial, the prosecution has the evidential burden to produce evidence on every element of the offence charged.

2. In order to discharge this burden, the prosecution must produce sufficient evidence to justify a conviction if that evidence were to remain unchallenged. In other words, the prosecution must establish a *prima facie* case (see *R v Galbraith* (1981)).

3. The court at the conclusion of the prosecution case will decide whether or not the evidential burden has been discharged. This process is sometimes referred to as 'passing the judge'.

2.4.2 The evidential burden on the accused at the close of the prosecution case

1. Once the prosecution has 'passed the judge' the evidential burden passes to the defence, but as it passes, the burden becomes less onerous.

2. If the prosecution fails to discharge its evidential burden, the accused will be entitled to be acquitted because the prosecution, by failing to produce evidence on every element of the offence charged, will be unable to discharge its legal burden of proof.

3. At the close of the prosecution case the accused is said to have an evidential burden because it is expected at that point in the trial that he will produce evidence in his defence. Failure to do so will not inevitably result in conviction.

2.4.3 The evidential burden where an accused raises a defence which goes beyond a denial of the prosecution case

A more onerous evidential burden falls on the accused where he relies on a defence which goes beyond a mere denial of the prosecution case. In that event, he must either produce evidence, or point to evidence already adduced by the prosecution, which raises the defence, or lays a proper foundation for the defence.

Examples of defences that go beyond a denial of the prosecution case:

- self-defence;
- duress;
- mechanical defect as the cause of an accident;
- reasonable excuse for failing to provide a breath test;
- provocation.

2.4.4 Evidential burden on accused where defence of non-insane automatism is relied upon

Because of the complex nature of this defence, the only way in which a proper foundation can be laid is by producing medical evidence in support. Failure to do so will result in the judge withdrawing the defence from consideration by the jury.

2.4.5 Duty of a judge to leave a defence to the jury: – the judge's 'invisible' burden

Where evidence emerges at trial suggesting the presence of a defence not raised by the defendant, the trial judge has a duty to leave this defence to the jury. This is sometimes referred to as the judge's 'invisible burden'. (see *R v Coutts* (2006) and *R v Foster* (2009)).

2.4.56 Presumptions

Presumptions may affect the operation of both legal and evidential burdens. Of at least some historical importance were the rebuttable presumptions of death, marriage and legitimacy: upon proof of certain primary facts, other secondary facts would be presumed in the absence of evidence to the contrary. Where rebuttable presumptions operate, then once the primary facts have been proved, the legal burden transfers to the other party. Presumptions are effectively rules of substantive law and their importance to a course on Evidence is merely tangential, hence the detail of these (and other) presumptions is excluded from this book.

A new species of presumption was created, however, under ss75 and 76 Sexual Offences Act 2003 which merits a mention. The terminology of the Act refers to evidential presumptions and conclusive presumptions. The presumptions relate to the duty on the prosecution in a sexual case to disprove consent.

1. Where an evidential presumption arises under s75, lack of consent will be presumed once the prosecution has proved certain primary facts, unless the defendant can rebut that presumption. On proof that the defendant had sexual intercourse with the complainant in a rape case, and that the defendant was aware at the time the sexual activity began, of the existence of the circumstances listed in s75(2), namely:

    ■ the use or fear of violence against the complainant or any person;
    ■ that the complainant was unlawfully detained;
    ■ that the complainant was asleep or unconscious;
    ■ that the complainant had a physical disability;
    ■ that a substance to stupefy or overpower the complainant had been administered,

    then lack of consent will be presumed unless the defendant can successfully rebut that presumption through evidence. The evidential presumption places the burden of adducing evidence on the issue of consent and the lack of *mens rea* on the defendant.

2. Where the presumption is conclusive under s76, once the prosecution has proved the required primary facts, lack of consent will be presumed, and the defendant cannot rebut the presumption. Lack of consent will be presumed, and that presumption cannot be rebutted by the defendant where:

    ■ the defendant intentionally deceived the complainant as to the nature or purpose of the relevant act; or
    ■ the defendant intentionally induced the complainant to consent to the relevant act by impersonating a person known personally to the complainant.

In *R v Jheeta* (2007) the Court of Appeal held that s76 will not apply if the victim knows the identity of the defendant and the purpose of intercourse is sexual gratification, even where the victim has been deceived in issues surrounding a relationship. Where the victim has been deceived and the purpose of the sexual act is not sexual gratification, then it is likely that s.76 will apply. In *R v Devonald* (2008) the defendant's purpose was humiliating the victim and s.76 applied.

2.5 The impact of the Human Rights Act 1998

1. Section 3(1) of the HRA 1998 requires judges and magistrates, so far as is possible, to construe legislation so as to give effect to the principles enshrined within the European Convention on Human Rights (ECHR).

2. Article 6(2) of the ECHR guarantees that any person charged with a criminal offence will be presumed innocent until the contrary is proved.

3. HRA 1998 has posed problems of construction for courts where legal burdens are imposed on defendants by statute, either expressly or by implication, under s101 of the Magistrates' Courts Act 1980.

2.5.1 Decisions on reverse burdens in the light of Article 6(2)

1. The European Court of Human Rights (ECtHR) in *Salabiaku v France* (1991) held that a reverse onus does not inevitably breach Article 6(2) but must be confined within reasonable limits which take into account the importance of what is at stake and maintain the rights of the defence.

2. In *R v Lambert* (2001) the House of Lords dismissed an appeal based on violation of Article 6(2) because the HRA 1998 had not been enacted at the time of trial. Despite finding that a literal interpretation of s28 of the Misuse of Drugs Act 1971 imposed a legal burden on the accused, a majority of the House held that s18 should be construed as imposing an evidential, rather than a legal burden.

3. The most recent, and therefore most authoritative decisions on reverse burdens are the conjoined appeals heard in the House of Lords, *Attorney General's Reference No 4 of 2002* and *Sheldrake v DPP* (2004). Having reviewed all the previous UK authorities, and many from other jurisdictions, the House of Lords identified a number of important points:

   ■ The interpretative obligation under s3 HRA 1998 is strong and may require a court to depart from Parliament's intention.
   ■ Where a Convention-compliant interpretation proves impossible the test for the courts to apply is whether a legal burden enacted by Parliament unjustifiably infringes the presumption of innocence. For

a reverse burden to be a justifiable infringement, the imposition of a legal burden must be proportionate.

In *Sheldrake*, the House of Lords held unanimously that the legal burden was on the appellant because the circumstances requiring proof by the appellant were clearly within his knowledge and easier for him to prove than for the prosecution. In *Attorney General's Reference No 4 of 2002* it was held that the burden imposed on defendants under s11(1) Terrorism Act 2000 is an evidential burden only, despite Parliament's obvious intention to impose a legal burden. Applying the 'justifiable and proportionate' test, the imposition of a legal burden on a defendant under s11(1) would be too onerous and the potential consequences of failing to discharge a legal burden too serious. This decision was by a 3:2 majority.

4. These cases establish that decisions on reverse burdens must be made on a case by case basis. Reverse burdens breach the presumption of innocence, but where a breach is both justifiable and proportionate, courts should give effect to Parliament's intention by imposing a legal, rather than an evidential burden on the defendant. In *R v Clarke (Roy)* (2008) the imposition of a legal burden on the defendant to prove he was qualified to provide immigration services under the Immigration and Asylum Act 1999, was justified and proportionate because: (1) it was much easier for him to prove qualification than for the prosecution; and (2) the offence created under the Act was designed to protect the public. In *DPP v Wright* (2009) it was held that exemptions in Schedule 1 of the Hunting Act 2004 did not impose a legal obligation on the defendant under s101 Magistrates' Court Act 1980, but simply an evidential burden and in *R v Keogh* (2007) obligations under the Official Secrets Act 1911, which appeared to impose a legal burden, were construed as imposing an evidential burden only.

2.6 The legal burden in civil cases

The legal burden in a civil case lies on the party who positively asserts the fact in issue and to whose claim or defence proof of that fact in issue is essential. In simple terms, he who asserts must prove.

1. Where it is not apparent from the papers which of the parties is making the positive assertion, the court may find that the legal burden lies with the party who would have least difficulty discharging that burden (*Soward v Leggatt* (1836); *Joseph Constantine Shipping v Imperial Smelting* (1942)).

2. Statute may decree which party bears the legal burden:
   - Under s98 Employment Rights Act 1996, where an employee claims unfair dismissal he has the legal burden of proving only that he was dismissed; the legal burden lies with the employer to prove that the dismissal was fair.
   - Under s171(7) Consumer Credit Act 1974, where a debtor claims that a credit bargain is extortionate the legal burden lies with the creditor to prove the contrary.
3. The legal burden may be fixed by agreement between the parties (*Chappell v National Car Parks* (1987)). Where the terms of the agreement are unclear, the courts will interpret the words of the agreement (*Hurst v Evans* (1917)).

2.7 The evidential burden in civil cases

1. The claimant (who makes a positive assertion and bears the legal burden at the start of the trial) also has the evidential burden.
2. At the close of the claimant's case the evidential burden passes to the defendant.
3. At the end of the trial the court must decide whether the **legal** burden has been discharged.

2.8 The standard of proof

1. There are two standards of proof: the criminal standard and the civil standard.
2. The standard of proof necessary to discharge the burden of proof relates to the legal, not the evidential burden.
3. The party who bears the legal burden on a particular issue will lose on that issue if the tribunal of fact considers the required standard of proof has not been reached.

2.8.1 The criminal standard of proof

1. Where the legal burden lies with the prosecution, the criminal standard of proof, beyond reasonable doubt, applies.

2. Where, exceptionally, the defendant bears a legal burden by raising a defence such as diminished responsibility or insanity, he need only discharge that legal burden to the civil standard, proof on a balance of probabilities (*R v Carr-Briant* (1943)).

3. Lord Denning, in *Miller v Minister of Pensions* (1947) explained the criminal standard: 'If the evidence is so strong against a man as to leave only a remote possibility in his favour … the case is proved beyond reasonable doubt'.

4. Judges must be careful in directing juries as to the meaning of the term 'proof beyond reasonable doubt'. The prudent judge will adopt the wording in *R v Summers* (1952) that the jurors must be 'satisfied so that they feel sure' where they feel an explanation of the term is necessary.

2.8.2 The civil standard of proof

Lord Denning, in *Miller v Minister of Pensions* (1947), said of the civil standard: 'If the tribunal of fact thinks it **more probable than not**, the burden is discharged'. A 51% probability is sufficient to discharge the civil burden of proof.

There are recognised exceptions to the general rule in civil cases where either the criminal standard or a standard higher than the normal civil standard of proof will be applied:

1. The standard of proof in committal proceedings for civil contempt of court is beyond reasonable doubt (*Dean v Dean* (1987)).

2. By virtue of a statutory requirement: for example under the Royal Warrant Act 1949, where an application is made for a war pension, the Minister must be satisfied beyond reasonable doubt that the claimant's application is not supported by the evidence before rejecting the application (*Judd v Minister of Pensions and National Insurance* (1966)).

3. Where a serious allegation of crime is made in the context of civil proceedings, it has been suggested that a higher standard of proof is appropriate (*Thurtell v Beaumont* (1923) and *Hornal v Neuberger Products Ltd* (1957)). In *R (N) v Mental Health Review Board (Northern Region)* (2006) it was made clear that there are only two standards of proof: the civil standard and the criminal standard. Richards LJ said 'the civil standard of proof is flexible in its application, and enables proper account of the seriousness of the allegations to be proved and the consequences of proving them' to be taken. This approach was also adopted by the House of Lords in *Re B (Children) (Sexual Abuse: Standard of Proof)* (2008).

4. Although the proceedings are civil in nature, the standard of proof applicable to the making of an anti-social behaviour order is the criminal standard. (*R (on the application of McCann) v Crown Court at Manchester* (2002)).

5. It has been held that evidence capable of rebutting the presumption of the validity of a marriage must be 'strong, distinct and satisfactory' *(Piers v Piers* (1849)) or even 'evidence which satisfies beyond reasonable doubt' *(Mahadervan v Mahadervan* (1964)).

3

Testimony of witnesses

3.1 Introduction

The most common form of presenting evidence to a court will be via live evidence. Witnesses will be called to give this form of evidence by both the prosecution and defence and in some cases witnesses can be forced or 'compelled' to come to court. If a witness is unwilling to testify, it is likely that a witness summons will be issued to secure his attendance. If he fails to attend court a warrant can be issued for his arrest and if he subsequently refuses to answer questions, he may be guilty of contempt of court.

3.2 Competence: general rule in criminal cases

1. All witnesses must be 'competent' to give evidence.

2. A witness is competent if, as a matter of law, a court can receive his evidence.

3. He is compellable if, as a matter of law, his refusal to testify may give rise to contempt proceedings (see *R v Yusuf* (2003)).

4. A witness who is competent will also be compellable unless he falls within an excepted category.

Statutory Authority: s53(1) of the Youth Justice and Criminal Evidence Act 1999: 'At every stage in criminal proceedings all persons are (whatever their age) competent to give evidence'.

3.2.1 Exceptions to the general rule in criminal cases

The accused:
- s1(1) CEA 1898
  s53(4) YJCEA 1999
  – incompetent as prosecution witness unless ceased to be accused

EXCEPTIONS TO THE GENERAL RULE ON COMPETENCE AND COMPELLABILITY IN CRIMINAL PROCEEDINGS

The spouse of the accused:
- s53(1) YJCEA 1999: competent
- s80(3) PACE 1984: limited compellability

Vulnerable witnesses (including children):
- unsworn evidence s55(2) YJCEA 1999
- special measures s16 YJCEA 1999

3.2.2 Public policy exceptions to the general rule

1. **The Sovereign** is competent but not compellable.

2. **Diplomats** are competent, but compellability is dependent upon statutory rules (including the Diplomatic Privileges Act 1964).

3. **Bankers** are compellable where the bank is a party to the proceedings, but not otherwise (s6 Bankers' Books Evidence Act 1879).

4. **The accused** is a competent witness in his own defence but is not compellable:

Statutory Authority: s1 of the Criminal Evidence Act 1898: '(1) A person so charged shall not be called as a witness in pursuance of this Act except upon his own application'.

The Accused is incompetent as a witness for the prosecution (s53(4) of the Youth Justice and Criminal Evidence Act 1999 (YJCEA 1999)) unless he is no longer liable to be convicted in the proceedings (s53(5)).

Where there are two or more defendants charged on the same indictment, one accused ceases to be a co-accused and becomes competent as a prosecution witness where:

    (a) proceedings are discontinued by the prosecution;

    (b) he is acquitted;

    (c) the indictment is severed and separate trials are directed;

    (d) one accused pleads guilty.

5. **The accused's spouse** (a person who is lawfully married or who has a contracted civil partnership under the Civil Partnership Act 2004) is competent and compellable for the defence unless jointly charged.

    (a) s/he is competent both for the prosecution (s53(1) and Schedule 4 of the YJCEA 1999) and a spouse's co-accused, but

    (b) s/he is not generally compellable unless the spouse is charged with an offence listed in s80(3) PACE 1984, namely:

- the offence involves an assault on, or injury or threat of injury to, the wife or husband or a person who was at the material time under the age of 16; or
- it is a sexual offence alleged to have been committed in respect of a person who was at the material time under the age of 16.
- the offence consists of conspiring or attempting to commit, or of aiding, abetting, counselling, procuring or inciting the commission of an offence involving an assault on the spouse or an assault or sexual offence against a person under 16.

    (c) Former spouses are competent and compellable for all parties (s80(5) PACE 1984).

    (d) Failure of a spouse to testify on behalf of a person charged shall not be the subject of comment by the prosecution (s80A PACE 1984).

3.2.3 Incompetence by virtue of personal characteristics

The presumption of competence under s53(1) of the YJCEA 1999 can be rebutted under s53(3):

'A person is not competent to give evidence in criminal proceedings if it appears to the court that he is not a person who is able to—

(a) understand the questions put to him as a witness; and

(b) give answers to them which can be understood'.

■ This section has particular relevance for witnesses of tender years and for those suffering from mental incapacity (see *R v D (Video Testimony)* (2002)).

■ Where the issue of competence arises, s54 of the YJCEA 1999 requires that the party seeking to call the witness must prove competence on a balance of probabilities.

■ In deciding whether the witness is competent, the judge will consider the effect of any 'special measures' to which the witness might be entitled under s16 of the Act (see 3.4 below).

■ Any questioning of the witness to determine competence must take place in the presence of the parties, but in the absence of the jury and the court is entitled to assistance from expert witnesses where appropriate.

3.3 Evidence: sworn, unsworn and solemn affirmation

1. A competent witness will give sworn testimony (or testimony given under a solemn affirmation) providing he is able to satisfy the requirements of s55(2) of the YJCEA 1999:

'The witness may not be sworn ... unless—

(a) he has attained the age of 14, and

(b) he has sufficient appreciation of the solemnity of the occasion and of the particular responsibility to tell the truth which is involved in taking an oath'.

2. Any competent witness who fails that test will be allowed to give unsworn testimony under s56 of the YJCEA 1999. As s55(2) makes clear, children under the age of 14 will automatically give their evidence unsworn, but the Act also allows adult witnesses to give unsworn testimony where they are unable to satisfy the test laid down by s55 (2).

3.4 Special measures

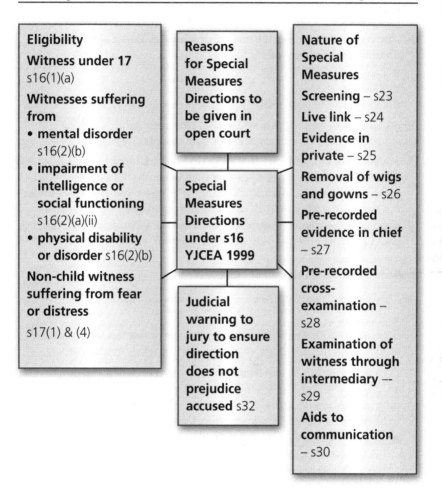

Eligibility

Witness under 17
s16(1)(a)

Witnesses suffering from
- mental disorder s16(2)(b)
- impairment of intelligence or social functioning s16(2)(a)(ii)
- physical disability or disorder s16(2)(b)

Non-child witness suffering from fear or distress
s17(1) & (4)

Reasons for Special Measures Directions to be given in open court

Special Measures Directions under s16 YJCEA 1999

Judicial warning to jury to ensure direction does not prejudice accused s32

Nature of Special Measures

Screening – s23

Live link – s24

Evidence in private – s25

Removal of wigs and gowns – s26

Pre-recorded evidence in chief – s27

Pre-recorded cross-examination – s28

Examination of witness through intermediary – s29

Aids to communication – s30

3.4.1 Eligibility for special measures

Witnesses who are 'eligible for assistance' in the form of special measures directions fall into three categories:

1. Witnesses under the age of 17 who are automatically eligible (s16(1)(a)).

2. Any witness the quality of whose evidence is likely to be diminished by reason of:
   - mental disorder (s16(2)(a)(i)); or

- significant impairment of intelligence or social functioning (s16(2)(a)(ii));
- a physical disability or disorder (s16(2)(b)).

3. Any non-child witness, the quality of whose evidence is likely to be diminished by reason of:
   - fear; or
   - distress,
   - in connection with testifying in the proceedings (s17(1)).

In the case of an adult victim of a sexual offence, eligibility will be presumed unless the witness declines assistance (s17(4)).

4. Students should be aware that ss 98–103 of the Coroners and Justice Act 2009 will make a number of important changes to the law on special measures. The most significant change will mean that witnesses under the age of 18, rather than 17, will automatically qualify as witnesses eligible for assistance. Sections 98–103 are not yet in force but students should monitor the position of this legislation.

3.4.2 Nature of special measures

The protections available for eligible witnesses are listed in ss22–30 of the Act:

1. **Screening** (s23): An eligible witness may be prevented from seeing the accused, but not the judge, justices or jury or legal representatives.

2. **Live link** (s24(8)): 'A live television link or other arrangement whereby a witness, while absent from the courtroom or other place where the proceedings are being held, is able to see and hear a person there and to be seen and heard [by the same persons as for screens]'.
   - In *R (on the application of D) v Camberwell Green Youth Court* (2003) the House of Lords held that the Human Rights Act 1998 and in particular Article 6 ECHR does not prevent a vulnerable witness from giving evidence via a live video link.
   - In *R (on the application of S) v Waltham Forest Youth Court* (2004) the Court of Appeal held that a vulnerable child defendant is not entitled to testify via video link since defendants are specifically excluded from entitlement to Special Measures under the Act.
   - Use of the live link was extended to defendants by s47 of the Police and Justice Act 2006 adding a new s33A to the YJCEA 1999. (see 3.4.2.9).

- Section 51 of the CJA 2003 also makes live links available to non-vulnerable witnesses in certain circumstances. (see 3.4.4).

3. **Evidence in private** (s25): Persons of 'any description' other than:
   (i) the accused;
   (ii) legal representatives;
   (iii) interpreters etc. assisting the witness;
   (iv) a single nominated and named representative of the press;
       may be excluded from the courtroom whilst the eligible witness is testifying. This protection is only available where:
   - the proceedings relate to a sexual offence; or
   - there are reasonable grounds for believing that some person other than the accused has sought or will seek to intimidate the witness while giving evidence (s25(4)).

4. **Removal of wigs and gowns** (s26).

5. **Evidence in chief by pre-recorded video** (s27): This is a very complex provision, but in outline, is as follows:
   (a) **Where the witness is under 17 at the time of hearing**:
   if the offence is sexual, or involves neglect, violence, kidnapping etc. (the full list of offences is set out in s21), the witness is deemed 'in need of special protection'. A video will take the place of live examination in chief unless:
   - facilities are not available; or
   - the court directs that all or part of the video should not be admitted in the interests of justice.

   Where the case is not one listed in s21 so that the child is not in need of special protection, the child's evidence will normally be by video, but there is an additional ground for directing live examination in chief under s21(4)(c) where the court is satisfied this is necessary to maximise the quality of the witness's evidence.

   (b) **Where the witness is over 17**:
   The court may make a direction for video-recorded evidence in chief unless it is of the opinion that it is not in the interests of justice (s27). Where that course is taken the witness must be called to give evidence under cross-examination at trial unless there is also:
   - a special measures direction for out of court cross-examination (s28, which authorises videoed cross-examinations is not yet in force); or
   - its admission is agreed.

6. **Video-recorded cross-examination and re-examination** (s28): This provision allows for mandatory cross-examination by video-recording for children under 17 who are 'in need of special protection' and discretionary video-taped cross-examination for children under 17 who are not in need of 'special protection' and for other 'eligible adult witnesses'.

   Section 28 is not yet in force.

7. **Examination of witness through intermediary** (s29): This provision permits the assistance of an interpreter or intermediary who is approved by the court. The provision is available whether the witness is giving evidence in person, via live link or by video recording.

8. **Aids to communication** (s30): An eligible witness may 'be provided with such device as the court considers appropriate with a view to enabling questions or answers to be communicated to or by the witness despite any disability or disorder or other impairment which the witness has or suffers from'.

9. **Vulnerable defendants and live video link** (s.33A): The defendant can apply to give evidence by live video link and in making its decision, the court must be satisfied that:

   where the accused is under 18 when the application is made:
   (a) his ability to participate effectively in the proceedings as a witness giving oral evidence is compromised by his level of intellectual ability or social functioning; and
   (b) use of a live link would enable him to participate more effectively in the proceedings as a witness (whether by improving the quality of his evidence or otherwise). (s33A(4)); or

   where the accused has attained the age of 18 at that time:
   (a) he suffers from a mental disorder (within the meaning of the Mental Health Act 1983) or otherwise has a significant impairment of intelligence and social function; and
   (b) he is for that reason unable to participate effectively in the proceedings as a witness giving oral evidence in court; and
   (c) use of a live link would enable him to participate more effectively in the proceedings as a witness (whether by improving the quality of his evidence or otherwise). (s33A(5)).

3.4.3 General points on special measures directions

1. An application for a Special Measures Direction is governed by Part 29 of the Criminal Procedure Rules 2010.

2. The Home Office has published 'Achieving Best Evidence' guidance to assist those making video recordings of evidence. It is important to follow this guidance as breaches will cause the court to consider 'could a reasonable jury properly directed be sure that the witness has given a a credible and accurate account ..., notwithstanding any breaches' (*R v K* (2006)).

3. Where the court makes a Special Measures Direction, s20(5) requires that reasons be given in open court. No application can be made to discharge a Special Measures Direction unless there has been a material change in circumstances.

4. Any evidence given by video-recording under a Special Measures Direction will form an additional exception to the rule against hearsay.

5. On a trial on indictment, the judge must give such warning to the jury, under s32: 'as s/he considers necessary to ensure that the fact that the direction was given in relation to the witness does not prejudice the accused'. This warning may be given as part of the judge's summing up, or, as suggested in *R v Brown* (2004), at the time the witness gives evidence.

3.4.4 Availability of live link to non-vulnerable witnesses

Section 51 CJA 2003 provides that a witness other than the defendant can testify by live link, if the court is satisfied it is in the interests of efficient or effective administration of justice and there are suitable facilities for receiving such evidence. This might allow a witness in one city to testify at a trial in another city without the need for attendance. Section 51 is currently only available in respect of certain sexual offences, (see Statutory Instrument 2007 No. 3451).

3.5 Anonymity of witnesses

1. Anonymity of witnesses is not included as a special measure under YJCEA 1999.

2. At common law there were a number of cases that established, in some circumstances, that witnesses could testify anonymously.

3. The House of Lords considered anonymity in *R v Davis* (2008). The appellant was convicted of murder. Three eye witnesses, accepted by the court to be in fear of their lives if their identity was known, testified under an extensive 'package' of measures concealing their identity. The question for the House of Lords was: whether '.. measures taken to preserve the anonymity of crucial witnesses in a criminal trial, hamper the conduct of the defence in such a manner and to such an extent that they were unlawful and rendered the trial unfair'. The ECtHR had stated in a number of cases that convictions should not be based solely or to a decisive extent on anonymous statements. Held: The measures adopted did not satisfy Article 6, as the conviction was based decisively on anonymous evidence and effective cross-examination was hampered.

4. Parliament's response to *R v Davis* (2008) was to pass the Criminal Evidence (Witness Anonymity) Act 2008 (the Act) roughly a month later which abolished the common law rules on anonymity. The speed of implementation led to a 'sunset clause' being included which expired on 31st December 2009. Anonymity of witnesses is now governed by ss86–90 of the Coroners and Justice Act 2009 which came into force on 1st January 2010.

5. Section 86 allows such specified measures as the court considers appropriate to ensure the identity of the witness is not disclosed and sets out a non-exhaustive list of those measures:
   (a) withholding the witness's name and other details;
   (b) use of a pseudonym;
   (c) a ban on asking questions which may identify the witness;
   (d) screening; and
   (e) voice modulation.

6. Section s86(2)(d) and (e) must not prevent the witness being seen and heard (without voice modulation) by the judge and jury.

7. Section 87 establishes both the prosecution and defence may apply for anonymity orders (note: where such an application is made by the defence, the witness's identity must be disclosed to the prosecution).

8. Section 88 establishes three conditions (a–c) that must be met before an anonymity order can be made:

A: The proposed order is necessary to protect the safety of the witness or another, prevent serious damage to property or prevent real harm to the public interest;

B: Having regard to all the circumstances, the effect of the proposed order would be consistent with the defendant receiving a fair trial; and

C: The importance of the witness's testimony is such that in the interests of justice the witness ought to testify; and

(a) the witness would not testify if the order was not made; or

(b) there would be real harm to the public interest if the witness were to testify without the proposed order being made.

9. Section 89(2) sets out considerations to which the court must have regard before deciding whether conditions A–C are met;

- ■ s89(2)(a) restates the importance of the common law principle that a defendant should know the identity of his accusers;
- ■ s89(2)(b)(d) and(e) deal with the credibility of witnesses;
- ■ s89(2)(c) establishes the need to consider the extent to which the witness's evidence 'might be the sole or decisive evidence' against the defendant;
- ■ s89(2)(f) asks the court to consider whether it would be possible to protect the witness's identity by any other means.

10. s90 establishes the judge must give the jury '"…such warning as … appropriate to ensure the making of the anonymity order does not prejudice the defendant'.

11. The Act was applied by the Court of Appeal in *R v Mayers* (2008). The appellant was convicted of murder, following a stabbing at a bus stop, on the basis of evidence provided by an anonymous witness about whom some 'disturbing facts' had been discovered. The witness was called late in the proceedings; had multiple previous convictions; was known to other witnesses and another man suspected of the crime and had come to the prosecution's attention via the victim's mother on the basis of information provided by another anonymised witness! The defendant's appeal was allowed because, when applying conditions A–C of the Act, the Court could not be sure of the credibility of the anonymous witness (s89(2)(b)(d) and (e)) whose 'evidence assumed decisive importance in the case' (s89(2)(c)). (Note: section numbers would have been those under the Act rather than those in the Coroners and Justice Act 2009).

3.6 Competence and compellability in civil proceedings: the general rule

1. In civil proceedings all adult witnesses are competent and compellable to give sworn evidence, including the claimant and the defendant.

2. Where one party challenges the competency of a witness, that issue will be determined at an early stage in the proceedings, usually pre-trial.

3.6.1 Exceptions to the general rule in civil proceedings

1. **Spouses**: under s1 of the Evidence Amendment Act 1853, a spouse is both competent and compellable in civil proceedings. It is doubtful whether the old case of *Monroe v Twistleton* (1802) remains good law, insofar as the case suggests that former spouses are incompetent in civil proceedings.

2. **Sovereigns and diplomats**: are competent but not compellable in civil proceedings.

3. **Bankers:** are competent but not compellable unless the bank is a party to the action.

4. **Children**: in civil proceedings a person under the age of 18 is regarded as a child (s105 of the Children Act 1989).
   (a) A child may give sworn evidence provided s/he is able to satisfy the test laid down in *R v Hayes* (1977) namely that:
   '… the child has sufficient appreciation of the solemnity of the occasion and the added responsibility to tell the truth, which is involved in taking an oath over and above the duty to tell the truth which is an ordinary duty of normal social conduct'.
   (b) In civil proceedings, if a child is unable to satisfy the *Hayes* test, then, by virtue of s96 of the Children Act 1989, s/he may give unsworn evidence if, in the opinion of the court:
   '(i) he understands that it is his duty to speak the truth; and
   (ii) he has sufficient understanding to justify his evidence being heard'.

5. **Mentally ill or mentally handicapped** witnesses will be competent to give sworn evidence provided they can satisfy the *Hayes* test; where a mentally ill or mentally handicapped witness is unable to satisfy that test he will be incompetent in civil proceedings.

4

Course of trial

Questioning of witnesses during the trial process is carried out in three stages: examination in chief, cross-examination and re-examination. Some rules of evidence are relevant purely at the examination in chief stage; others apply only in cross-examination.

Examination in chief

Refreshing the memory from documents (ss139 and 120 CJA 2003):
- statement made by witness whilst events fresh in mind;
- witness does not remember matters referred to and could not reasonably be expected to do so.

Previous consistent statements inadmissible except:
- s120 CJA 2003: Recent complaints by victims of crime;
- rebutting suggestions of recent fabrication;
- res gestae/previous identification;
- statement in response to accusation.

Unfavourable and hostile witnesses:
- s3 Criminal Procedure Act 1865.

Cross-examination

Previous inconsistent statements:
- ss 4 and 5 Criminal Procedure Act 1865.

Cross-examination of police officers on conduct in other cases:
- s100(1)(a) CJA 2003.

Finality rule on collateral questions:
- s6 Criminal Procedure Act 1865;
- bias;
- medical evidence of disability.

Sexual offences:
- ss41–43 YJCEA 1999.

Re-examination

Previous consistent statement admissible in rebuttal.

4.1 Examination in chief

The purpose of examination in chief is for the party calling the witness to take the witness through his evidence and extract facts favourable to his case. No leading questions are permitted.

4.1.1 Refreshing the memory from documents

1. This is now governed by s139 CJA 2003:

   'A person giving oral evidence in criminal proceedings about any matter may, at any stage in the course of doing so, refresh his memory of it from a document made or verified by him at an earlier time if—
   (a) he states in his oral evidence that the document records his recollection of the matter at that earlier time, and
   (b) his recollection of the matter is likely to have been significantly better at that time than it is at the time of his oral evidence'.

   ■ Note that under s139 there is no longer a need for contemporaneity, as previously required at common law. The judge will be in the best position to decide whether the witness's recollection was likely to have been better at the time of making the statement and such a decision should be accepted unless it is 'unreasonable' or 'perverse' (*R v McAfee* (2006)).

2. Under s120(3): 'A statement made by the witness in a document—
   (a) which is used by him to refresh his memory while giving evidence,
   (b) on which he is cross-examined, and
   (c) which as a consequence is received in evidence in the proceedings is admissible as evidence of any matter stated of which oral evidence by him would be admissible'.

   ■ This replaces the previous common law rule that where a witness referred to a previous document, that document was allowed only as an *aide-mémoire*. Today the document is admissible as evidence of any matter stated.
   ■ The jury will not be entitled to retire with copies of the statement unless the court considers it appropriate, or all parties agree to them being available (s134 CJA 2003).

4.1.2 Refreshing the memory in civil proceedings

1. Witnesses may refresh their memory from proof of evidence or from notes before entering the witness box.

2. Under s6(4) and (5) Civil Evidence Act 1995 (CEA 1995), where new issues are raised during cross-examination that were not referred to in chief, the memory-refreshing document may be admitted as evidence.

3. At common law a witness may refresh his memory from a document made contemporaneously with the events referred to providing:
   ■ The document was made or verified by the witness whilst the events were fresh in his memory;
   ■ The document is produced for inspection by the court and the other parties.

4. A non-contemporaneous document may be referred to in the course of testimony where the witness is unable to recall the events referred to and the document was made closer to the events in question (*R v Da Silva* (1990)).

5. Where a document used to refresh memory is admitted under s6(4) and (5) CEA 1995 it is relevant to the credibility of the witness and is admissible as evidence of any fact stated within it.

4.2 Previous consistent statements

Statements from the witness box to the effect that a similar account has been given on a previous occasion are inadmissible in both criminal and civil proceedings (*R v Roberts* (1942)). This is sometimes referred to as the rule against narrative. There are exceptions to this general rule.

4.2.1 Exceptions

1. **Section 6(4) and (5) CEA 1995**: in civil cases, with leave of the judge, a witness can refer in chief to a previous consistent statement. No leave is required where the purpose of adducing such evidence is to rebut a suggestion that the evidence has been fabricated.

2. **Section 120 CJA 2003** allows the admission of evidence of recent complaints made by victims of crime. This considerably broadens the previous common law, which allowed evidence of complaints in sexual cases only. The relevant provisions allow for the admission of a previous statement by the witness providing (i) the witness indicates that, to the best of his belief, he made the statement; (ii) he indicates that to the best of his belief the statement is true; and (iii) that the conditions in s120(7) are satisfied:
   's120(7) …

(a) the witness claims to be a person against whom an offence has been committed,

(b) the offence is one to which the proceedings relate,

(c) the statement consists of a complaint made by the witness (whether to a person in authority or not) about conduct which would, if proved, constitute the offence or part of the offence,

(d) (this sub-section, which required the complaint to be made as soon as could reasonably be expected after the alleged conduct, has been repealed by the Coroners and Justice Act 2009);

(e) the complaint was not made as a result of a threat or a promise; and

(f) before the statement is adduced the witness gives oral evidence in connection with its subject matter'.

Subsection (8) establishes that a complaint remains admissible even where it is elicited as the result of a leading question, providing no threat or promise was involved.

3. Evidence of complaints made by victims of crime may also contain **details of a victim's distress**. Such distress reinforces the victim's credibility and has probative value but judges should warn juries to take care with this sort of evidence as it can easily be feigned (see *R v Chauhan* (1981)).

4. **Previous consistent statements** may be admissible as part of the *res gestae* (*R v Fowkes* (1856)) (see 8.4).

5. **Previous identification**: evidence that a positive identification has previously been made can be given either by the witness, or by a third party who witnessed the identification.

6. **Previous statements made in response to accusations**: where an accused is challenged about incriminating acts and makes a statement exonerating himself that statement will normally be admissible, even though it is essentially self-serving.

   ■ The justification for this exception is explained by Lord Widgery in *R v Storey* (1968): 'A statement made voluntarily by an accused person to the police is evidence in the trial because of its vital relevance as showing the reaction of the accused when first taxed with the incriminating facts ... the statement is not strictly evidence of the truth of what was said, but is evidence of the reaction of the accused which forms part of the general picture to be considered by the jury at the trial'.

- In *R v Tooke* (1990), Lord Lane explained the test to be applied in deciding admissibility. It is 'partly that of spontaneity, partly that of relevance, and partly that of asking whether the statement which is sought to be admitted adds any weight to the other testimony which has been given in the case'.

4.3 Unfavourable and hostile witnesses

- An unfavourable witness is one who does not come up to proof yet acts in good faith.
- A hostile witness is one who does not wish to tell the truth.
- It is for the judge to decide whether a witness is unfavourable or hostile.

4.3.1 Dealing with unfavourable and hostile witnesses in criminal proceedings

1. Where a witness is merely unfavourable the party calling that witness can attempt to nullify the effect of his evidence through other evidence but cannot cross-examine the unfavourable witness.

2. Where the party calling a witness believes that witness to be hostile, then he may seek leave to treat the witness as hostile. If granted, the party who called the witness can:
   (a) contradict his evidence through other evidence; or
   (b) under s3 of the Criminal Procedure Act 1865, cross-examine the witness on his previous inconsistent statement.

3. Where a previous inconsistent statement is admitted under s3 Criminal Procedure Act 1865, then, by virtue of s119 CJA 2003, that statement 'is admissible as evidence of any matter stated in it of which oral evidence by that person would be admissible'. This is an important change: prior to CJA 2003, a previous consistent statement was relevant only to credibility, so the effect of admitting a previous inconsistent statement was to eradicate the evidence of that witness. As a result of s119, the tribunal of fact may prefer and act upon the evidence in the previous statement rather than that of the witness during the course of trial.

4.3.2 Unfavourable and hostile witnesses in civil proceedings

1. In civil proceedings a previous inconsistent statement can be used either to discredit the witness's oral testimony, or as evidence in the case. This rule replicates the position in criminal cases under s119 CJA 2003.

2. Even where a witness is merely unfavourable, leave may be sought to introduce a previous inconsistent statement under s6 CEA 1995.

4.4 Cross-examination

1. The purpose of cross-examination is to extract favourable facts from witnesses called by the other party and cast doubt on the opponent's case.

2. Questioning is not restricted to matters raised in chief and leading questions are permitted.

3. Any matters in dispute must be put to the witness, or it will be assumed that the facts, as stated by the witness are true.

4. In a criminal trial involving several defendants, each has the right to cross-examine all witnesses.

5. Sections 34–36 YJCEA 1999 restrict a defendant's right to cross-examine. Section 34 prevents cross-examination by the defendant in person of a complainant in a sexual case; s35 prevents cross-examination by the defendant of a child witness in a sexual case, or one involving kidnap, false imprisonment, child abduction or assault; and s36 allows a judge to prohibit cross-examination by the accused where such a course is likely to improve the quality of a witness's evidence and where it would not be contrary to the interests of justice to make such a direction. Where the defendant is prevented from cross-examining a witness under ss34–36 YJCEA 1999, he or the court will be given the opportunity to appoint a representative to conduct the cross-examination on his behalf.

4.4.1 Previous inconsistent statements

1. Any discrepancy between a previous statement and oral evidence can be put to witnesses in cross-examination (ss 4 and 5 of the Criminal Procedure Act 1865).

2. Under s119 CJA 2003 a previous inconsistent statement is admissible as evidence of any matter stated in it so where a witness is cross-examined on such a statement, the tribunal of fact may prefer and act upon the previous statement in preference to the witness' evidence at trial.

3. In civil proceedings (s6(1) CEA 1995) the judge can be asked to prefer the previous statement to the oral evidence.

4.4.2 Cross-examining police officers on other cases

Prior to the coming into force of CJA 2003, the cross-examination of police officers about their conduct in other cases was governed by case law, the most important guidelines being laid down in *R v Edwards* (1991):

■ The acquittal of a defendant in Case A, where the prosecution case depended largely or entirely on the evidence of a police officer, did not normally render that officer liable to cross-examination as to credit in Case B.

■ However, where Case A resulted in an acquittal in circumstances where a jury must have disbelieved a police officer's evidence relating to a disputed admission, then in Case B, where an admission was similarly disputed, it was considered proper that the jury should be made aware of the earlier case.

■ However, where the acquittal in Case A did not 'necessarily' indicate that the jury disbelieved the officer, such cross-examination would not be allowed. A verdict of not guilty need not necessarily mean that the jury believed that a police officer had lied in evidence.

It would seem that evidence that a previous jury verdict was **consistent** with perjury would not be sufficient.

Following the coming into force of CJA 2003, cross-examination of police officers in such circumstances is regarded as cross-examination on bad character. As such, cross-examination will be governed by s100 CJA 2003. Where the defence wishes to cross-examine a police officer about his conduct in a previous case he will have to satisfy the court that the questions amount to 'important explanatory evidence' under s100(1)(a), or that his alleged misconduct has 'substantial probative value in relation to a matter which is a matter in issue in the proceedings, and is of substantial importance in the context of the case as a whole' (s100(1)(b)) (see 7.4). Where the conduct of a police officer does not fall within the definition of bad character in ss98 and 112 CJA 2003 (see 7.3) then the admission of the evidence will be subject to the test of relevance and the common law rules will apply.

4.4.3 Collateral questions and the finality rule

1. Collateral questions will normally, though not invariably, relate to the credit of the witness being cross-examined.

2. The general rule is that collateral questions may be asked, but the answer given by the witness must be treated as final.

3. Collateral questions were defined in *Attorney-General v Hitchcock* (1847): if a piece of evidence could have been introduced had the witness not given evidence, it is not collateral. If that evidence could not have been introduced in the absence of the witness, it is collateral.

4. An alternative test, which is easier to apply, is:

> Does the question relate solely to the witness rather than to a fact in issue? If the answer is 'yes', then the question is collateral.

Example

R v Burke (1858): an Irish witness gave evidence through an interpreter, having stated that he spoke no English. In cross-examination it was suggested he had spoken to two people in court in English. He denied that suggestion. That answer had to be treated as final since the witness's ability to speak English was not a fact in issue in the case. The question was admissible, but being collateral, was subject to the finality rule.

4.4.4 Exceptions to the finality rule

1. **Section 6 Criminal Procedure Act 1865**: All witnesses can be asked if they have any criminal convictions recorded against them (with the exception of the accused).

2. **Bias**: Where an allegation of bias is made against a witness, a denial need not be treated as final (see *R v Mendy* (1976); *R v Phillips* (1936); *R v Busby* (1982).

3. **Medical evidence of disability**: For example, an eye witness can be questioned about any eye-condition which might affect the quality of

his testimony. See *Toohey v Metropolitan Commissioner of Police* (1965) for a slightly unusual example.

4.5 Cross-examining complainants in sexual cases on previous sexual history

1. Protection is provided to complainants in sexual cases from cross-examination on previous sexual history by s41(1) YJCEA 1999, which provides:

   'If at a trial a person is charged with a sexual offence, then, except with the leave of the court

   (a) no evidence may be adduced, and

   (b) no question may be asked in cross-examination by or on behalf of any accused at the trial, about any sexual behaviour of the complainant'.

2. 'Sexual behaviour' is defined in s42(1)(c) as:

   'any sexual behaviour or other sexual experience, whether or not involving any accused or other person, but
   excluding ... anything alleged to have taken place as part of the event which is the subject matter of the charge against the accused'. Thus cross-examination of the complainant about pre-offence behaviour towards the accused is allowed insofar as it forms part of the events leading up to the offence.

3. Section 41(4) states:

   'No evidence or question shall be regarded as relating to a relevant issue in the case if it appears to the court to be reasonable to assume that the purpose (or main purpose) for which it would be adduced or asked is to establish or elicit material for impugning the credibility of the complainant as a witness'.

4. Note that s41 prohibits cross-examination on previous sexual history. It does not prevent evidence relating to previous sexual history from being admitted as part of the prosecution case (see *R v Ball* (2005) at 7.5.5 below).

4.5.1 The power to grant leave under s41(2)

1. Leave to cross-examine a complainant on previous sexual history may be granted in only four very limited circumstances:

(a) **Where the issue is not one of consent** (s41(3)(a)). Cross-examination may be allowed where the defence is that the offence never took place, or, more worryingly, where the accused genuinely or mistakenly believed that the victim was consenting.

   ■ s42(1)(b) defines *issue of consent* as:
   'any issue whether the complainant in fact consented to the conduct constituting the offence with which the accused is charged (and accordingly does not include any issue as to the belief of the accused that the complainant so consented)'.

(b) **Where the issue is one of consent and the behaviour occurred around the same time as the alleged offence** (s41(3)(b)):
   '[the sexual behaviour of the complainant] to which evidence or question relates is alleged to have taken place at or about the same time as the event which is the subject matter of the charge against the accused'. The explanatory notes to the YJCEA 1999 state that 'at or around the same time' should be interpreted to mean either 24 hours before or after the alleged incident (see also *R v A (No .2)* (2002)).

(c) **Where the issue is one of consent and the sexual behaviour is so similar** (s41(3)(c)) to either:
   '(i) any sexual behaviour of the complainant which (according to evidence adduced or to be adduced by or on behalf of the accused) took place as part of the event which is the subject matter of the charge against the accused, or
   (ii) any sexual behaviour of the complainant which … took place at or about the same time as that event, that the similarity cannot reasonably be explained as a coincidence'.

■ Under this limb, the sexual behaviour may take place over a wider timeframe than in s41(3)(b) but the behaviour must in some way or other be so striking that it is relevant to consent.

■ This exception has been dubbed the 'Romeo and Juliet' scenario because the balcony scene provides a useful illustration. If the circumstances of an alleged rape involved the defendant climbing to a balcony and having intercourse with the complainant, his defence being that she had invited him to do so, evidence that she had similarly invited other men on previous occasions to climb to the balcony for the purposes of intercourse might well be admissible under this limb.

The scope of this paragraph has been extended by the House of Lords in *R v A (No. 2)* (2002) to allow leave to be given where there has been a previous consensual relationship between the defendant and the complainant.

(d) **Evidence of sexual behaviour adduced by the prosecution** (s41(5)). This subsection permits leave:

'(i) [where the evidence or question] relates to any evidence adduced by the prosecution about any sexual behaviour of the complainant; and

(ii) in the opinion of the court, would go no further than is necessary to enable the evidence adduced by the prosecution to be rebutted or explained by or on behalf of the accused'.

Cross-examination will be allowed under s41(5) so long as a prosecution witness's assertion was not deliberately elicited by the defence (*R v Hamadi* (2007)).

2. Even where one of the four exceptions above applies, leave may only be granted subject to the following provisos:

■ 'A refusal of leave might have the result of rendering unsafe a conclusion of the jury or (as the case may be) the court on any relevant issue in the case' (s41(2)(b)).

■ Leave may never be granted under the first three limbs 'if it appears to the court to be reasonable to assume that the purpose (or main purpose) … is to establish or elicit material for impugning the credibility of the witness' (s41(4)).

■ The evidence or questioning must relate only to specific instances of sexual behaviour (s41(6)). Thus evidence of reputation can never be allowed in evidence (see *R v White* (2004) at 4.5.2.5).

3. Section 41(5) allows the defendant the opportunity to introduce evidence of previous sexual conduct to rebut an assertion made by the prosecution. Where, for example, the complainant was presented to the jury as a virgin at the time of the alleged rape, it would be open to the defence to introduce evidence in rebuttal of that assertion.

4.5.2 Case law on ss41 and 42

1. The HRA 1998 threatens to undermine the protection afforded to complainants under s41 YJCEA 1999. The case of *R v A (No 2)* (2001), decided by the House of Lords, raises a number of important issues as the House struggled to construe ss41–43 in accordance with the requirements of Article 6 of the ECHR, the right to a fair trial.

■ Their Lordships held that a purposive approach to the construction of s41, as required under s3 of the HRA 1998, should be adopted.

Admissibility was dependent upon relevance to the issue of consent, but trial judges must be satisfied before granting leave that excluding such evidence would breach the right to a fair trial.

■ Although the appeal related specifically to s41(3)(c), their Lordships provided useful guidance on s41(3)(a) and (b). Under s41(3)(a), which allows leave to cross-examine to be granted where evidence is relevant to an issue other than consent, Lord Hope identified a number of circumstances that might satisfy this paragraph. These included:

(i) where the accused relies on a defence of honest belief in consent;

(ii) where allegations of bias or fabrication are made against the complainant.

■ Under s41(3)(b), which allows leave to be granted where evidence relates to sexual behaviour 'at or about the same time' as the alleged rape, Lord Steyn suggested that evidence relating to an invitation to have sex earlier on the same evening would satisfy the provision; and Lord Hope suggested that the phrase might properly be interpreted as encompassing conduct which occurred several minutes to several hours before the alleged rape. He thought it unlikely that an incident occurring several days before could be construed as 'at or about the same time'.

■ On s41(3)(c) Lord Hope concluded that the test was not satisfied on the facts as there was no similarity with the complainant's sexual behaviour on a previous occasion. Section 41 was designed to prevent cross-examination on the basis that because the complainant had had consensual intercourse on a previous occasion she was more likely to have consented on this occasion. The onus, in those circumstances, is upon the defendant to demonstrate that the similarity in the complainant's behaviour cannot be explained on the grounds of coincidence. Importantly, s41(3)(c) was identified as the means for admitting evidence of previous sexual relationship between the complainant and the defendant.

2. In *R v T; R v H (Complainant's Sexual History)* (2001) the defendants were prevented under s41 from cross-examining the complainant (i) on her failure to mention the alleged conduct when reporting to the police alleged abuse by other men; and (ii) by asking questions designed to demonstrate a pattern of lying in relation to sexual and non-sexual matters. The Court of Appeal held that s41 must be given a purposive interpretation. Questions directed at the complainant's credibility were

not automatically prohibited under s41(4) and in this instance should have been allowed.

3. In *R v E* (Dennis Andrew) (2004) the appellant appealed against convictions for indecent assault against his two daughters, aged 6 and 4 at the time of the trial. Some 15 months after the trial, whilst living with foster parents, the children made allegations of indecent assault against other people and the appellant applied to cross-examine them about these complaints on the basis that they were unlikely to be true, and cast doubt upon the credibility of their videotaped interviews at his trial. The appellant wished to question the children as to their understanding of sexual matters. The Court of Appeal held that it was unlikely that Parliament had intended for children to be cross-examined on their perception of sexual matters in order to determine whether the protection afforded by s41 applied, and the appeal was dismissed.

4. In *R v Martin* (2004) M denied raping V on Wednesday. At trial he was refused leave to cross-examine V on whether she had pestered him for sex and performed a sex act on him the previous Monday. M claimed his rejection of her advances on that occasion motivated her invention of the rape allegation on the Wednesday. The Court of Appeal held that cross-examination on events relating to the Monday would indeed have impugned the credibility of the complainant, which would contravene s41(4), but that leave should have been given in this case because the main purpose of the cross-examination was not to impugn her credibility but to establish his own defence (see also *R v F* (2005)).

5. In *R v White* (2004), D was held to have been correctly prevented from cross-examining the complainant as to whether, at the time of the alleged rape, she was still working as a prostitute. The questioning did not relate to specific instances of sexual behaviour.

4.5.3 Procedural points

1. Applications for leave are heard in private in the absence of the complainant (s43(1)).

2. The court must state reasons for granting or refusing leave in open court in the absence of any jury and specify the extent of the leave granted (s43(2)).

3. Applications for leave are governed by Rule 36 Criminal Procedure Rules 2010.

4.6 Re-examination

1. The purpose of re-examination is for the party calling the witness to restore the credibility of that witness and emphasise points favourable to his case.

2. Questions in re-examination are normally restricted to matters raised in cross-examination.

3. Whilst evidence of a previous consistent statement is inadmissible in chief, it may be allowed in re-examination to rebut an assertion made in the course of cross-examination. Where, for example, it is suggested to a witness in cross-examination that his evidence is a recent fabrication, that allegation can be rebutted by introducing evidence in re-examination relating to a previous consistent statement.

4. No new evidence can be introduced once the jury has retired (*R v Gearing* (1966)).

5

Corroboration, lies, care warnings and identification evidence

CORROBORATION OR JUDICIAL WARNINGS

Judicial warning to take care required

disputed identification evidence (*R v Turnbull* (1977)).

Corroboration required by statute:

s89(2) Road Traffic Act 1984;

s13 Perjury Act 1911;

s1 Treason Act 1795.

Judicial direction required:

lies told by accused (*R v Lucas* (1981));

alibi defence raised by accused (*R v Burge, Hurst and Pegg* (1996)).

Discretionary warning to take care

where evidential basis for believing witness' evidence might be 'suspect'.

5.1 Introduction: The general rule

1. 'Corroboration' is generally unnecessary in England and Wales. A court can act on the unsupported testimony of one witness or one document, even where other evidence contradicts that evidence.

2. At common law, very complex rules had evolved requiring corroboration of certain categories of evidence before that evidence

could be acted upon; other evidence required a warning to the jury to take care before relying upon uncorroborated evidence.

3. As a result of the Criminal Justice and Public Order Act 1994 (CJPOA 1994), the requirement for corroboration in its legal sense has almost entirely been eradicated. Despite that Act a limited number of exceptions remain, hence it is still necessary to understand the nature of corroboration.

5.1.1 The limited requirement for corroboration

1. Section 32(1) of the CJPOA 1994 states that:

'Any requirement whereby at a trial on indictment it is obligatory for the court to give the jury a warning about convicting the accused on the uncorroborated evidence of a person merely because that person is

(a) an alleged accomplice of the accused, or

(b) where the offence charged is a sexual offence, the person in respect of whom it is alleged to have been committed, is hereby abrogated'.

2. As a result of s32(1), corroboration in its strict legal sense is relevant today only in those circumstances (detailed in 5.1.3) where there can be no conviction in the absence of corroboration.

5.1.2 Legal definition of corroboration

1. The legal definition was laid down by Lord Reid CJ in *R v Baskerville* (1916):

'Evidence in corroboration must be independent testimony which affects the Accused by connecting him or tending to connect him with the crime. In other words it must be evidence which implicates him, that is which confirms in some material particular not only that the crime has been committed, but also that the prisoner committed it'.

2. It must therefore:

(i) be admissible in itself;

(ii) derive from a source independent of the witness whose evidence needs corroborating; and

(iii) show not only that the crime was committed, but that it was committed by the Accused.

5.1.3 Statutory corroboration required

Corroboration is required by statute in three situations:

1. **Exceeding the speed limit**: s89(2) Road Traffic Act 1984: 'A defendant cannot be convicted of exceeding a speed limit on the opinion evidence of one witness'.

   ■ If the police rely on an instrument, such as a speed gun or speedometer reading, a single police officer can give evidence, as it is a matter of fact (not opinion) that the machine registered a particular speed (*Brighty v Pearson* (1938)).

2. **Perjury**: under s13 Perjury Act 1911:

   'A person shall not be liable to be convicted of any offence against this Act, or of any offence declared by any other Act to be perjury or subornation of perjury, or to be punishable as perjury or subornation of perjury solely upon the evidence of one witness as to the falsity of any statement alleged to be false'.

3. **Treason**: s1 Treason Act 1795 provides that a person cannot be convicted of high treason, which involves the death or kidnap of the Queen or her heirs, without the oaths of two credible witnesses. The Criminal Law Revision Committee recommended the repeal of this statutory requirement as long ago as 1972.

5.1.4 Care warnings – suspect witnesses

1. Under s32(1) CJPOA 1994 a judge has a discretion, not a duty, to warn the jury to take care before relying upon the evidence of any witness where he is satisfied that there is an evidential basis for so doing.

2. Lord Taylor CJ laid down guidelines relating to the circumstances in which discretionary warnings should be given in *R v Makanjuola* (1995):

   (a) Whether or not a warning is given, and the nature of such a warning, are matters of judicial discretion in all cases. A warning may, but need not be given in respect of accomplices testifying for the prosecution and complainants in sexual cases, as is the position with any other witness. It will depend on the circumstances of the case, the issues raised and the quality of the witness's evidence.

   (b) A warning to take care before relying on a witness's evidence should not be given merely because a witness is a complainant in a sexual case or an accomplice. There must be some other aspect of the evidence, such as lying, previous false complaint, or bias before such a warning is given.

(c) Warnings should be given as the judge reviews the evidence in the course of his summing up rather than as a separate legal direction.

(d) Although the substance of each warning is discretionary, judges should avoid repeating the old and technical corroboration warning.

(e) The Court of Appeal will be slow to interfere with the exercise of a judge's discretion unless that exercise is unreasonable in the *Wednesbury* sense.

3. There is no requirement on a judge to direct the jury as to which evidence is and is not capable of amounting to corroboration in the technical *Baskerville* sense.

4. According to *R v B (MT)* (2000) he should nevertheless identify to the jury any 'independent supporting evidence'. Such evidence might be found in lies told by the accused either in court or pre-trial (see 5.2 below), the silence of the accused (ss34–37 CJPOA 1994 (see 6.2)), or admissions made by the accused during the course of testimony that support the prosecution case.

5. In *R v G (Terry)* (2002), G appealed against his conviction for rape and indecent assault alleged to have been committed against T when she was between 4 and 8 years old. When interviewed on video T contended that her brother and sister had witnessed some incidents but they made no reference to this in their evidence. The appeal was allowed because the trial judge gave no warning to the jury advising special caution.

6. In *R v Charalambous* (2009) C, who was convicted of robbery, alleged that M and S had placed him under duress to commit the offence as he owed them a gambling debt. They were called to give evidence by the prosecution to rebut this assertion. In the course of his summing up the judge acknowledged the possibility that this could have been a joint enterprise and that M and S were fortunate not to be sitting in the dock! The Court of Appeal found that the judge had not erred in failing to exercise his discretion and give a warning to the jury to take care when considering the evidence of M and S, because the need to exercise such caution was 'perfectly obvious'.

5.2 Lies told by the accused

1. Lies told by a defendant may be probative of guilt and may support other evidence.

2. Wherever the prosecution proposes to rely upon the lies of a defendant, a *Lucas* direction should be given to the jury. The judge must direct the jury that a lie may be probative of guilt only where each of four conditions, laid down in *R v Lucas* (1981) are satisfied:

   (a) The lie must be deliberate;

   (b) It must relate to a material issue;

   (c) The motive must be a realisation of guilt and fear of the truth;

   (d) It must be clearly shown to be a lie by admission or independent evidence.

3. A modern version of the test, which expands its application to alibi defences, was laid down in *R v Burge, Hurst and Pegg* (1996). A direction is normally required where:

   - the defence raises an alibi;
   - the judge considers it desirable or necessary to suggest that the jury should look for support of a piece of evidence (e.g. disputed identification evidence), and draws attention specifically to lies told or allegedly told by the accused;
   - the prosecution suggests that something said in or out of court was a lie, and relies on that lie as evidence of guilt;
   - although the prosecution does not seek to rely on a lie as evidence of guilt, the judge believes there is a danger that the jury might do so.

4. The direction should include two points:

   (i) the jury must be satisfied that the lie is either admitted or proved beyond reasonable doubt; and

   (ii) they must be reminded that the mere fact the accused lied is not itself evidence of guilt since the accused might lie for innocent reasons; only if the jury is convinced that the lie was told for no innocent reason could such a lie support the prosecution case.

5. In *R v Barnett* (2002) the judge did not give a *Lucas* direction to the jury despite B giving a number of conflicting accounts as to why there was a stolen painting, worth in the region of £40,000, under his bed. The Court of Appeal found that just because the defendant had made inconsistent statements did not mean the jury would necessarily infer guilt. The evidence did not fall within one of the categories in *R v Burge, Hurst and Pegg* (1996).

5.3 Identification evidence

Identification evidence has long been regarded as potentially unreliable. In 1976, following a number of notorious miscarriages of justice, a Committee, chaired by Lord Devlin, considered necessary reform. Their recommendations were given effect in *R v Turnbull* (1977) and by Codes of Practice issued under the Police and Criminal Evidence Act 1984. The latest version of the Code was published in February 2008.

5.3.1 Safeguards at a pre-trial stage

Police officers should consider which method of identification is most appropriate in each case. Four procedures are regarded as acceptable, depending on the circumstances:

   (i) video identification;
   (ii) identification parade;
   (iii) group identification;
   (iv) confrontation.

1. The preferred method of identification today is the video identification now used in 98% of cases.

2. Whatever form of identification procedure is selected, police officers must record a description from the witness before the procedure takes place. This description must be disclosed to the defence before trial.

3. Where police have a suspect available, witnesses should not be shown photographs. Where no suspect is available and photographs are shown, at least 12 images should be included in the bundle.

   ■ In *R v Sutton* (2002) the Court of Appeal quashed the conviction of S who had been identified by a police officer by means of video identification. The officer had a photograph of S in his possession immediately before making the identification.

4. Identification evidence, like any other prosecution evidence, is subject to exclusion under s78 PACE 1984 where the Court believes its inclusion would adversely affect the fairness of the proceedings. Exclusion may be the consequence where major breaches of Code D have occurred.

5.3.2 When should an identification procedure take place?

1. *R v Forbes* (2001) clarified the circumstances in which an identification parade must be held. It was stressed that the provisions of Code D were mandatory and additional unwritten conditions must not be inserted. Where a suspect disputes a witness's identification and consents to a parade, then a parade must be held.

2. Code D states that where there is a disputed identification, an identification procedure should be held 'unless it is not practicable or it would serve no useful purpose in proving or disproving whether the suspect was involved in committing the offence'.

3. Where a witness claims he would be unable to identify an offender, there is no requirement to hold an identification parade, despite a request from the suspect (*R v Nickolson* (1999)).

4. Where a witness provides a description of an offender but does not identify him, there is no need to hold an identification procedure (*R v Oscar* (1991)).

5.3.3 Video identification

1. Annex A of Code D regulates this procedure, which is quite similar to the identification parade.

2. The parade is organised by an 'identification officer' who has no direct involvement with the case. The officer will use the Video Parade Electronic Recording System (VIPER) to produce the parade.

3. The film must include eight 'stooges' who, so far as possible, resemble the suspect. The suspect and his lawyer should be given an opportunity to view the film prior to the witness and they can make 'reasonable objections' to the film. If practicable, steps are taken to remove the objection. The suspect's solicitor will be given the opportunity to be present when the video is shown to the witness. The suspect is not entitled to be present. If this does not occur, then the procedure must be recorded on video.

4. As with the identification parade, there must be no opportunity for witnesses to communicate with each other.

5. A breach of the procedures laid down by the Codes will not necessarily affect the admissibility of identification evidence (*R v Coddington* (2005)).

6. In *Perry v United Kingdom* (2004) the European Court of Human Rights found that Article 8, respect for private life, had been violated where the applicant was covertly filmed for the purposes of identification when he attended a police station. The interference with Article 8 was unlawful as the police had failed to comply with the PACE 1984 Codes of Practice Code D para D.2.11, para D.2.15 and para D.2.16 by not informing him that he was being filmed or obtaining his consent to that activity.

5.3.4 Identification parades

1. Annex B of Code D governs the conduct of an identification parade. Briefly, some of the important paragraphs require:
   (a) the officer conducting the parade should not be involved in the case;
   (b) the suspect must be told of his right to have a solicitor or friend present;
   (c) the parade must be photographed or videoed, and everything said and done should take place in the presence and hearing of the suspect or his representative;
   (d) where no representative is present, the parade must be videoed; in any event the procedure must be video-recorded or a colour photograph taken;
   (e) at least eight 'stooges' must take part and they should resemble the suspect as far as possible;
   (f) the suspect can select his own position in the line-up;
   (g) the suspect is entitled to make 'reasonable objections' to the way in which the parade is organised or to any of the 'stooges' and steps are taken, if practicable, to remove the objection;.
   (h) witnesses should be brought into the room where the parade takes place individually and there should be no opportunity for witnesses to communicate with each other.

5.3.5 Group identification

1. This involves a witness viewing the suspect amongst an informal group of people.

2. The procedure may take place with the consent and co-operation of a suspect or covertly where a suspect refuses to co-operate with other procedures, or where the officer in charge of the investigation believes

this form of identification is more satisfactory than an identification parade or video identification.

3. Annex E of Code D requires that a colour photograph be taken of the scene immediately after the identification is made.

5.3.6 Confrontation

1. When no other method of identification is available, confrontation may be used (*R v Kelly* (2003)).

2. This will normally take place in a police station, with the witness being asked, 'Is this the person?'

3. It is, for good reason, regarded as the least reliable form of identification.

4. In *R v Jones and Nelson* (1999) both defendants refused to take part in an ID parade and officers organised a confrontation. Jones refused to co-operate and covered his head with clothing. This was forcibly removed. The whole incident was watched by the witness through a viewing panel. The Court of Appeal quashed the convictions on the grounds that evidence obtained by means of a forced confrontation should have been excluded.

5.4 Safeguards at trial

Guidelines, which apply in every criminal case involving disputed identification evidence, were established in *R v Turnbull* (1977). These are:

1. The judge must issue a warning to the jury to take care before relying upon identification evidence. This should take place in any case involving disputed identification evidence and should include an explanation of the reasons why caution is necessary.

2. The judge should direct the jury to look closely at the circumstances in which the identification took place: the lighting, distance, time for observation etc.

3. The judge should point out to the jury any weaknesses in the identification evidence. Were there, for example, any discrepancies between the description initially supplied by the witness and the appearance of the defendant?

4. The judge must consider the quality of the identification evidence: if the quality is good, then the case can be left for the jury to consider

providing that a *Turnbull* warning is given; if the evidence is poor then the judge must withdraw the case from the jury unless there is supporting evidence. In *R v Galbraith* (1981) it was emphasised that on a submission of no case to answer, a case should be withdrawn only where there is no evidence or where that evidence is so tenuous that a properly directed jury could not convict.

5. The judge should identify any evidence that supports the reliability of the identification evidence.

5.4.1 The nature of supporting evidence

1. Lord Widgery suggested in *R v Turnbull* (1997) that a failure by the accused to testify at trial, or a refusal to answer questions at the police station, could not amount to supporting evidence. That situation has changed as a result of ss34–37 CJPOA 1994 (see 6.2). Silence can provide support for disputed identification evidence, as can lies told by the accused and false alibis, subject to the required *Lucas* direction. Evidence admitted under the 'bad character' provisions in s100(1) CJA 2003 (see 7.5.2) can also be used to support identification. In *R v Isichei* (2006), I was identified by the complainant as the man who had robbed her. The complainant gave evidence that shortly before the robbery I had shouted at her that he wanted his 'coke' back. The prosecution was allowed to use I's previous conviction for having been concerned in the importation of cocaine, admitted under s101(1)(d), to provide support for the complainant's identification. Circumstantial evidence in a case can also provide support for a disputed identification. In *R v Sadler* (2002) identification was supported by the defendant having a shirt soaked in the blood of the victim.

2. Supporting evidence is that which tends to support or confirm other evidence. It need not amount to corroboration under the old *Baskerville* test. Judges should identify to jurors evidence that is capable of providing support; whether or not such evidence does provide support is a matter for the jury to decide.

5.4.2 The circumstances in which a *Turnbull* warning must be given

1. Case law suggests that the safest course is to deal with all cases of disputed identification evidence in accordance with the *Turnbull* guidelines. Failure to apply the guidelines is likely to result in convictions being quashed on appeal (see *Reid v The Queen* (1990)).

2. There is no special wording for formulating *Turnbull* directions, providing that the sense and spirit of the guidelines is complied with (*Mills v R* (1995)).

3. Although recognition evidence is regarded as less dangerous than identification of a stranger, a *Turnbull* warning remains necessary (*R v Bentley* (1991)).

4. *R v Thornton* (1995) suggests that where the accused admits his presence at the scene, but denies participation in the events that led to the charge, a full *Turnbull* warning is required.

5. In *R v Slater* (1995) *Thornton* was distinguished: where presence at the scene is admitted, and the distinctive appearance of the accused eradicates the danger of an eye witness mistakenly identifying the wrong person, no *Turnbull* warning is necessary.

6. A warning is inappropriate, according to *R v Clements* (2004), where the defendant admits his presence at the scene and the only issue relates to the credibility of the witness' account as to the defendant's conduct.

7. In *R v Gayle* (1999) the appellant was convicted of burglary following the theft of a handbag from a school. The offender was seen at a distance by the school caretaker who provided a description of his clothing. The appellant was seen by a cook disposing of the bag in a bin at a local public house. He admitted disposing of the bag, but claimed he found it and denied burglary. The Court of Appeal held that there was no need for a *Turnbull* warning on these facts since there was no disputed identification evidence. The appellant did not dispute the cook's identification of him; and the caretaker did not purport to identify anyone: he merely provided a description.

5.4.3 Voice recognition

1. Where an offender is purported to have been identified through voice recognition rather than visual identification, *R v Hersey* (1998) and *R v Roberts* (2000) suggest that an appropriately adapted *Turnbull* warning must be given. In *R v Robinson* (2005) the Court of Appeal approved the test laid down by the trial judge: where voice recognition evidence is adduced by a co-accused, providing it is relevant and probative, the judge has no discretion under s78 PACE 1984 to exclude the evidence. The basic test for admissibility is low: 'Is the evidence such that no reasonable jury properly directed as to its defects could place any weight upon it?'

2. The courts have drawn a distinction between non-expert voice identification given by those familiar with the voice in question (often a police officer) and the expert evidence of a forensic scientist with expertise in this area. In *R v Flynn and St. John* (2008) the Court of Appeal quashed two convictions based on the 'self-evidently very prejudicial' voice identification evidence of four police officers. The police officers' identifications were based on their experience of the appellants' voices, despite an expert witness being unable to identify the comments referred to as 'words' or distinguish between the voices on the tape.

6

Silence: drawing adverse inferences against the defendant

6.1 Introduction

1. By virtue of ss34–37 CJPOA 1994, a jury is entitled to draw whatever inferences are proper from the failure of an accused to testify at trial, failure to mention when questioned or charged matters which are later relied on at trial, or failure to account for incriminating evidence.

2. As a result of the Criminal Procedure and Investigations Act 1997, as amended by CJA 2003, adverse inferences can also be drawn from failure to comply with disclosure requirements (see 13.8.4).

6.2 Silence under the Criminal Justice and Public Order Act 1994

s34	s35
Failure to mention when questioned any fact relied on at trial	**Refusal to testify or failure to answer questions at trial**

Inferences that can be drawn from silence under CJPOA 1994

s36	s37
Failure to account for objects, substances or marks	**Failure or refusal to account for presence at the scene**

A couple of important points relating to all four sections are:

- The sections do not make an accused person compellable in the technical sense of the term; under s35, failure to testify will not lay him open to contempt proceedings.
- A person cannot be convicted of an offence solely on the basis of an inference drawn from silence (s38(3)). The court or jury must be satisfied that the prosecution has established a *prima facie* case before inferences may be drawn.

6.2.1 s35 of the Criminal Justice and Public Order Act 1994

1. This section allows the court to draw such inferences as appear proper from the defendant's failure to give evidence or his refusal, without good cause, to answer any question at the trial (s35(3)).

2. The court must be satisfied that the accused is aware that the stage has been reached at which evidence can be given for the defence and that, if he chooses not to give evidence, inferences can be drawn (s35(2)).

3. The section does **not** apply where:
   (a) the accused's guilt is not in issue; or
   (b) it appears to the court that the physical or mental condition of the accused makes it undesirable for him to give evidence (see *R v Friend (No. 2)*(2004)).

6.2.2 Judicial guidance on s35

1. Lord Taylor CJ, in *R v Cowan* (1996) advised that courts should decline to draw adverse inferences, or advise a jury against drawing such an inference from silence at trial only where there is 'some evidential basis for doing so or some exceptional factors in the case making that a fair course to take'.

2. The Judicial Studies Board has published specimen directions on s35, the gist of which are that judges must direct the jury that:
   - the accused is entitled to remain silent;
   - silence alone is not sufficient to justify a conviction;
   - the jury should consider any explanation for his silence and should draw inferences only where they conclude that silence must, sensibly, be attributed to the defendant having no answer.

6.2.3 s34 of the Criminal Justice and Public Order Act 1994

1. Similar inferences can be drawn under s34 where an accused fails to mention when questioned following caution or charge, facts which he later relies upon in his defence.

2. The substance of s34 is reflected in the words of the caution so the accused is effectively put on notice whenever the caution is administered:

   'You do not have to say anything. But it may harm your defence if you do not mention when questioned something which you later rely on in court. Anything you do say may be given in evidence'.

3. Note that it is not only a refusal to answer questions when interviewed which may lead to inferences being drawn under s34; inferences can be drawn where the suspect does answer questions but fails to mention 'a fact which in the circumstances existing at the time the accused could reasonably have been expected to mention when so questioned, charged or informed …'.

4. Section 58 YJCEA 1999 has amended ss34, 36 and 37 by inserting new ss34(2A), 36(4A) and 37(3A) which provide that the adverse inference provisions will not apply:
   - if the accused was not at an 'authorised place of detention' (a police station) at the time of his failure or refusal; and
   - if he was not allowed the opportunity of consulting a solicitor.

5. Where no specific defence is relied on at trial, the jury must be directed not to draw adverse inferences under s34 (*R v Moshaid* (1998)).

6. Section 34 inferences may be drawn only where the defendant relies on facts he might reasonably have been expected to mention during interview. Questions that invite an accused to suggest an innocent explanation for prosecution evidence will not bring s34 inferences into play. In those circumstances, he has not relied upon a defence; he has merely theorised at the invitation of prosecuting counsel (*R v Nickolson* (1999); *R v B* (MT) (2000)).

7. In deciding whether or not to draw adverse inferences under s34, the court is obliged to consider the circumstances existing at the time. According to *R v Argent* (1997), this phrase encompasses the state of mind of the accused, his level of intelligence, command of English, and knowledge of the facts surrounding the offence.

8. Where an accused remains silent on the basis of legal advice from his solicitor, this will not necessarily prevent the jury being directed to consider whether an inference can be drawn. The legal advice is a 'very relevant' circumstance that the jury should consider when looking at the reasonableness of the accused's conduct in all the circumstances which the jury have found to exist' (*R v Argent* (1997)). Case law and the specimen direction produced by the Judicial Studies Board make it clear that inferences may be drawn where a defendant is hiding behind the advice rather than relying on it in a genuine way (see *R v Betts and Hall* (2001) and *R v Howell* (2005)).

9. A 'simple statement' at trial or during interview that the failure to answer questions was based on legal advice will not waive legal professional privilege (*R v Bowden* (1999)). In *R v Wishart; R v Boutcher* (2005) the defendant claimed he had maintained silence during interview on legal advice and raised an undisclosed alibi at trial. The judge asked during cross-examination whether the defendant had informed his advising solicitor of his alibi defence and the defendant claimed he had. The judge held he had waived privilege and ordered disclosure of the solicitor's notes. The Court of Appeal quashed his conviction holding that the appellant had not waived privilege by strenuously denying the prosecution's allegation that he had recently fabricated his alibi defence by asserting that he had told his solicitor. In *R v Loizou* (2006) it was held that where privilege is waived the extent to which disclosure will be permitted is subject to a test of 'fairness'. The court will consider whether failing to disclose additional material will create a misleading impression for the jury. (see also 13.4).

10. In *R v Bresa* (2005) the Court of Appeal reviewed both the authorities and the guidelines issued to judges by the Judicial Studies Board when directing juries under s34. The focus of the decision was on silence following legal advice. Students would benefit from reading this judgment in its entirety.

11. Where the accused declines to answer police questions but submits a pre-prepared statement giving an account which corresponds with his evidence at trial, this will prevent inferences being drawn under s34 (see *R v Knight* (2003)).

6.3 Human rights and adverse inferences

1. The first case involving silence provisions to reach the ECtHR was *Murray v United Kingdom* (1996). On the facts of the case it was found that there was no breach of Article 6(1) or (2), but it was suggested there might well have been breaches had the accused been denied access to legal advice. The court stressed the importance of accurate and fair jury directions involving inferences from silence (this was not a problem in *Murray* since that trial took place before a Diplock court, where a judge sits without a jury).

2. In *Condron v United Kingdom* (2001) the ECtHR held that there had been a violation of Article 6(1): the right to a fair trial. It was emphasised that appeal courts must consider the fairness of trials, not just the safety of convictions, and *Condron* was distinguished from *Murray* on two grounds:

   - In *Condron* the defendants had given evidence at trial and explained why they had refused to answer questions at the police station (their solicitor formed the view that the appellants were suffering withdrawal symptoms and were unfit to be interviewed).
   - *Condron* was a jury trial and since juries are not required to give reasons for their verdicts, directions in the course of a judge's summing up are vital.

7

Character and convictions

7.1 Overview of character provision in CJA 2003

Non-defendants	
Good character	**Bad character**
Inadmissible where purpose to enhance credibility (*R v Robinson* (1994))	Admissible under s100(1) CJA 2003 only if:
	(a) it is important explanatory evidence
	(b) it has substantial probative value re a matter in issue, and is of substantial importance in the context of the case.
	(c) all parties agree to its admission.

LIMITED ADMISSIBILITY OF EVIDENCE RELATING TO CHARACTER IN CRIMINAL PROCEEDINGS

Defendants	
Good character	**Bad character**
Admissible, and relevant (i) to credibility and (ii) to issue of guilt or innocence (*R v Vye* (1993))	Admissible under s101(1) CJA 2003 only if:
	(a) all parties to the proceedings agree
	(b) evidence is adduced by the defendant himself
	(c) it is important explanatory evidence
	(d) it is relevant to an important matter in issue between defendant and prosecution
	(e) it has substantial probative value re an important matter in issue between defendant and co-defendant
	(f) it is evidence to correct a false impression given by the defendant
	(g) the defendant has made an attack on another person's character

1. The admission of good character evidence is regulated by common law rules.

2. The admission of bad character evidence is regulated entirely by ss98–112 CJA 2003.

3. The procedure for admitting evidence of bad character is governed by Part 35 Criminal Procedure Rules 2010 which imposes notice requirements, time limits and a procedure for objection.

4. CJA 2003 provides protection for non-defendants: bad character evidence can be admitted only through three gateways provided by s100 CJA 2003. Under the pre-CJA 2003 law, bad character of non-defendants was always admissible under s6 Criminal Procedure Act 1865 (CPA 1865).

5. For defendants, bad character evidence is regulated purely by CJA 2003 with such evidence only being admitted through seven gateways in s101(1) CJA 2003. Previous common law rules, including rules on similar fact evidence, and statutory provisions under s1(3) Criminal Evidence Act 1898 (CEA 1898) are now abolished.

6. Similar fact evidence rules remain relevant in civil cases and have influenced interpretation of s101(1)(d) CJA 2003 in criminal cases.

7.2 Good character

The rules for admission of good character evidence are different for defendants and non-defendants.

7.2.1 Good character of non-defendants

1. Evidence designed to enhance the credibility of a non-defendant is inadmissible (*R v Robinson* (1994)).

2. Evidence that merely has the effect of enhancing credibility will not necessarily be excluded. In *R v DS* (1999) the complainant to a sexual offence allegedly committed some years previously, stated in evidence that he was a Church of England clergyman. The Court of Appeal applauded the judge's direction in summing up the case to the jury that although they might take the witness's profession into account, they should concern themselves primarily with the impression he made on them in the witness box.

7.2.2 Good character of defendants

1. The accused may always adduce evidence of his own good character although precisely what the term 'good character' means is not entirely clear. In *R v Rowton* (1865) the court held that evidence of good character is limited to the 'general reputation of the accused in the community'.

2. The accused is entitled to present himself as a person without previous criminal convictions as established by *R v Vye* (1993). Having reviewed the authorities, the Court of Appeal ruled that good character is relevant both to credibility and to the issue of guilt or innocence. Guidelines were provided to judges summing up cases to juries:

   ■ Where a defendant is of good character and testifies on his own behalf, the trial judge must direct the jury that the defendant's good character is relevant to his credibility as a witness.

   ■ Where a defendant of good character does not testify at trial, but relies on exculpatory statements made to the police or others, the judge must direct the jury to have regard to the defendant's good character when considering the credibility of those statements.

   ■ Where a defendant does not testify at trial and has made no exculpatory statements at a pre-trial stage, then no direction on the relevance of his good character to credibility need be given because his credibility is not in issue.

   ■ Whether or not a defendant testifies on his own behalf, a direction must be given to the effect that the defendant's good character is also relevant to the issue of guilt or innocence.

3. Where two or more defendants are tried together and only one is of good character the defendant without convictions remains entitled to a *Vye* direction. Whether or not the judge makes reference to the character of a co-accused with previous convictions is a matter of judicial discretion: the judge may decide to say nothing or may direct the jury not to speculate about the character of the co-accused since they have heard no evidence on the matter.

4. Trial judges have a discretion to qualify the *Vye* direction in the interests of common sense. In *R v Aziz* (1995) the House of Lords confirmed that a judge should never be compelled to give meaningless or absurd directions, and that the *Vye* direction could be qualified in the light of admitted misconduct.

5. Where previous convictions are 'spent' under the Rehabilitation of Offenders Act 1974 a defendant will normally be entitled to a full *Vye*

direction (*R v Heath* (1994)), however judges retain a discretion to adapt the direction where that is appropriate, perhaps by directing jurors that the defendant has no 'relevant' convictions (*R v O'Shea* (1993)).

6. Problems arise where a defendant is technically entitled to both 'good' and 'bad' character directions. Trial judges should consider modifying the bad character direction to inform the jury that the defendant would normally be entitled to a good character direction, owing to his lack of criminal record and explain the relevance of this to both guilt and credibility (*R v Doncaster* (2008)).

7.3 Definitions under the CJA 2003

Bad character under s98 CJA 2003:

'References … to evidence of a person's "bad character" are to evidence of, or a disposition towards, misconduct on his part, other than evidence which—

(a) has to do with the alleged facts of the offence with which the defendant is charged, or

(b) is evidence of misconduct in connection with the investigation or prosecution of that offence'.

1. Bad character, under s98, is a wider concept than criminal convictions: it includes 'a disposition towards misconduct', or propensity.

2. Section 98 excludes from the ambit of the Act evidence which:
   - 'has to do with the alleged facts of the offence' (e.g. evidence relating to the theft of a car used in a bank robbery at the defendant's trial for robbery); and
   - 'evidence of misconduct in connection with the investigation or prosecution of that offence' (e.g. evidence that the defendant resisted arrest).

   By excluding such evidence from the Act, the pre-CJA 2003 position is retained: the evidence may be admissible at common law, subject only to relevance. In *R v Machado* (2006) the appellant, M, appealed against his conviction for robbery. M wanted to inform the court that the alleged victim had told him he had taken an ecstasy tablet and that he had offered to sell him drugs. The trial judge held this was inadmissible as it was evidence of bad character. The Court of Appeal found the evidence was 'to do with the alleged facts of the offence' and was not bad character for the purposes of s98 CJA 2003.

Misconduct under s112(1) CJA 2003:

'the commission of an offence or other reprehensible behaviour'.

---

3. 'Other reprehensible behaviour' may cause some problems of interpretation: presumably it covers conduct that is considered morally blameworthy, such as adultery, or a poor disciplinary record in the workplace or sporting environment (see *R v Marsh* (1994)) where evidence of a poor disciplinary record on the rugby field was admitted in a case of assault against a man with no criminal convictions).

4. The Explanatory Notes accompanying the CJA 2003 suggest that 'misconduct' might include evidence that a person has a sexual interest in children or is a racist.

5. In *R v Manister* (2005), the 39-year-old appellant, M, had been convicted on three counts of indecent assault against a 13-year-old complainant, A. The trial judge admitted evidence of a consensual sexual relationship between M and a 16-year-old girl. The Court of Appeal upheld the convictions. The previous consensual relationship did not constitute bad character under s98 and its admission is therefore dependent on common law. In this case it was admissible because it was relevant to the issue whether M had a sexual interest in A, since it showed he had an interest in teenage girls much younger than him.

6. In *R v Osbourne (Gary)* (2007) the Court of Appeal found evidence of the appellant's history of shouting at his partner, if he failed to take his medication for schizophrenia, not to be 'reprehensible behaviour' for the purposes of CJA 2003. Some element of culpability or blameworthiness is required.

7.4 Bad character of non-defendants

1. Prior to the enactment of CJA 2003, witnesses could always be cross-examined on previous convictions either at common law or under s6 CPA 1865. Such evidence was regarded as relevant to the credibility of the witness.

2. The admission of bad character evidence relating to a non-defendant is now regulated by s100(1) CJA 2003, which provides three gateways for the admission of bad character evidence as defined by s98.

> **Gateways for the admission of bad character evidence of non-defendants under s101(1) CJA 2003:**
>
> (a) it is important explanatory evidence;
>
> (b) it has substantial probative value in relation to a matter which:
>
>   (i) is a matter in issue in the proceedings, and
>
>   (ii) is of substantial importance in the context of the case as a whole; or
>
> (c) all parties to the proceedings agree to the evidence being admissible.

Leave of the court is required before evidence can be admitted under (a) or (b).

3. The term 'important explanatory evidence' (s100(1)(a)) is clarified by s100(2):

'(a) without it, the court or jury would find it impossible or difficult properly to understand other evidence in the case; and

(b) its value for understanding the case as a whole is substantial'.

4. Section 100(3) identifies factors that must be considered in assessing whether evidence has 'substantial probative value' under s100(1)(b):

- the nature and number of events, or other things, to which the evidence relates;
- when those events or things are alleged to have happened, or existed;
- in the case of evidence of misconduct that is said to have probative value by virtue of its similarity between that conduct and other alleged misconduct, the nature and extent of the similarities and dissimilarities between each of the alleged instances of misconduct;
- in the case of misconduct, when it is alleged that the person is also responsible for the offence charged, and the identity of the person responsible for the misconduct is disputed, the extent to which evidence shows or tends to show that the same person was responsible each time.

Example

Where a defendant is charged with murder and claims that a prosecution witness, not himself, committed that murder, it is likely that evidence relating to previous instances of violence committed by the witness on the complainant would be admitted. That evidence would have a substantial probative value in relation to an issue in the case and would be of substantial importance in the context of the case as a whole.

5. The Court of Appeal has indicated evidence of a witness's bad character may be admitted for the purposes of undermining their credibility as a witness and to demonstrate propensity to act in a particular way.

■ In *R v Osbourne* in the appeals of *R v Renda et al* (2005) the appellant had been convicted of a robbery at a public house. The appellant argued that no robbery had occurred and the landlord had fabricated the allegation to cover up for his own misconduct. A defence witness, W, supported the appellant's claim that no robbery had taken place. W had a recent conviction for an offence of serious violence and the Crown wanted to cross- examine him about this under s100(1)(b). The Court of Appeal held that evidence of W's bad character was of substantial probative value in relation to his credibility as a witness on the vital question as to whether a robbery had actually taken place. W's previous conviction was admitted under s100(1)(b).

■ In *R v S (Andrew)*(2006) the appellant, S, appealed against his conviction for indecent assault on a prostitute. S claimed the complainant had consented to perform sex acts for an agreed fee, but then demanded more money, threatened to accuse him of rape and tried to steal his gold chain. The trial judge refused to allow the defence to cross-examine the complainant on her previous convictions, for a variety of dishonesty offences, on the basis that they damaged her credibility. The Court of Appeal agreed with the trial judge but found the complainant's previous offending had substantial probative value in relation to her propensity to behave in the way the appellant claimed.

7.4.1 Previous convictions of non-defendants: s74(1) PACE 1984

1. In criminal proceedings the conviction of someone other than the accused is admissible under s74 PACE 1984 as evidence of the facts upon which it is based where it is relevant to an issue in the case to prove that a person committed an offence. This might include admitting evidence of the guilty plea of a person jointly charged (see *R v Dixon* (2000)) or evidence of A's conviction for theft at B's trial for handling stolen goods.

2. Note that the required relevance relates to any issue in the proceedings and not necessarily the question of the guilt of the accused. Where the prosecution proves relevance, the judge is required to consider whether to exercise his discretion to exclude evidence under s78 PACE 1984.

3. Guidelines on the application of s74 were provided by the Court of Appeal in *R v Mahmood and Another* (1997). The court must apply a two-fold test:
   - whether the conviction is clearly relevant to an issue in the trial (the prosecution must identify the issue in respect of which the conviction is relevant);
   - if relevant, whether there would be prejudice to the defendant(s) in respect of the fairness of the proceedings.

4. The modern trend is to restrict the use of s74, and where convictions are admitted under this section, the judge must direct the jury on the relevance of the conviction in very careful terms (*R v Dixon* (2000)).

7.5 Bad character of defendants

1. Bad character evidence relating to a defendant is regulated by s101(1) CJA 2003. This subsection provides seven gateways through which bad character evidence can be admitted.

Seven gateways for the admission of bad character evidence of defendant under s101(1):

(a) all parties to the proceedings agree to the evidence being admitted;

(b) the evidence is adduced by the defendant himself or is given in answer to a question asked by him in cross-examination and intended to elicit it;

(c) it is important explanatory evidence;

(d) it is relevant to an important matter in issue between the defendant and the prosecution;

(e) it has substantial probative value in relation to an important matter in issue between the defendant and a co-defendant;

(f) it is evidence to correct a false impression given by the defendant; or

(g) the defendant has made an attack on another person's character.

2. Section 101(1)(a) and (b) are relatively uncontentious: where an accused appreciates that his bad character is admissible under another gateway, he may choose to introduce that evidence himself in order to suggest he is being wholly frank in his testimony to the court.

7.5.1 Section 101(1)(c): Important explanatory evidence

1. 'Important explanatory evidence' is defined in s102 in identical terms to those used in s100(2) (see 7.4). It is adduced, not because it is directly relevant to a fact in issue, but to provide the background necessary for the court to properly understand the evidence. Evidence admissible under gateway (c) would include:

■ evidence of events that occurred close in time, place or circumstance to the offence charged;

■ evidence necessary to complete an account of the circumstances of the offences charged so as to make it comprehensible to a jury;

■ evidence of a previous relationship between the defendant and the alleged victim of the offence charged;

■ evidence to establish motive.

2. Case law is helpful in providing examples of how s101(1)(c) operates. Some of the pre-CJA 2003 case law remains relevant:

■ In *R v TM* (2000), nine defendants were charged with 43 counts of sexual abuse. Evidence was admitted relating to the grooming by parents of their son, who was encouraged firstly to watch the abuse of his sister, and secondly to participate in the abuse. It was held that without this evidence the jury could not fully have appreciated the significance of other evidence.

■ In *R v P (Mark Geoffrey)* (2006) the appellant had been convicted of the attempted rape of his partner and appealed against the trial judge's decision to introduce evidence of his bad character under s101(1)(c). The appellant admitted the relationship with his partner was volatile, but although he did not object to a previous conviction for common assault on her going before the jury, he objected to the prosecution introducing evidence of seven previous incidents of violence, one where the complainant alleged she was raped. Because the appellant had given evidence of the nature of the relationship, the Court of Appeal found it was important for his partner to have the opportunity to do so. The value of the evidence to the jury in understanding the case was substantial.

■ In *R v Beverley* (2006) the Court of Appeal held the appellant's conviction for conspiracy to import cocaine was unsafe owing to the admission of previous convictions for possession of cannabis and possession with intent to supply cannabis under s101(1)(c) CJA 2003. The Court of Appeal was unable to see why the jury would have been disadvantaged in understanding the evidence linking the defendant with the crime without the convictions before them.

■ In *R v D* (2008) the Court of Appeal stated the test in s102 CJA 2003 should be applied cautiously particularly where there is an 'overlap' with 'propensity' evidence admissible under s.101(1)(d), in view of the more restrictive approach of s101(1)(d) and safeguards for exclusion under s101(3).

3. It is possible that evidence of previous acquittals may be admitted in some circumstances under s101(1)(c). In *R v Cerovic* (2001) the appellant was convicted on three counts of making threats to kill and one of harassment. The appellant telephoned his former girlfriend threatening to repeat what he had done two years previously, when he had taken a gun to the victim's sister's house and, during a struggle, he shot her. The appellant was acquitted of attempted murder and possession of a firearm in respect of the shooting, but it was important explanatory evidence regarding the appellant's state of mind and the fear of the victims in the current trial.

7.5.2 Section 101(1)(d): Important matter in issue between defendant and prosecution

1. Section 101(1)(d) is the widest, the most complex and potentially the most far-reaching gateway. To be admissible, evidence must be relevant either to a fact in issue or to the credibility of the defendant.

2. There is no requirement for the 'substantial probative force' necessary to admit evidence of bad character relating to a non-defendant.

3. The phrase 'matters in issue between the defendant and the prosecution' is partially explained by s103(1). Such matters include:
   '(a) the question whether the defendant has a propensity to commit offences of the kind with which he is charged, except where his having such a propensity makes it no more likely that he is guilty of the offence;
   (b) the question whether the defendant has a propensity to be untruthful, except where it is not suggested that the defendant's case is untruthful in any respect'.

4. Evidence of 'propensity to commit offences of the kind with which he is charged' may be demonstrated by proving that the defendant has previously been convicted of an offence either of the 'same description or the same category' as the one with which he has been charged (s103(2)).

   ■ An offence of the same *description* is one that would have been written in the same terms in the charge or indictment (s104(4)(a)), e.g. where a defendant is charged with rape and has a previous conviction for rape, that conviction may be admissible to show he has a propensity to commit offences of the kind with which he is charged, 'except where his having such a propensity makes it no more likely that he is guilty of the offence' (s103(1)(a)).

   ■ Offences of the same category are defined by the Secretary of State (s103(4)(a)). Two categories of offence have so far been prescribed: (i) Theft, and (ii) Sexual Offences (persons under the age of 16). Within the Theft category are offences of theft, burglary or aggravated burglary where the intention is to steal, robbery, taking a motor vehicle without consent, aggravated vehicle taking, handling stolen goods, going equipped for stealing and making off without payment. The Sexual Offences category is equally wide, covering rape, intercourse with a girl under 16, indecency, sexual assault and a whole range of other offences committed on persons under the age of 16.

5. In *R v Hanson, Gilmour and Pickstone* (2005), Rose LJ emphasised that establishing merely that offences are of the same description or the same category as the offence charged is insufficient to show propensity. He proposed a set of three questions to determine admissibility:

   (i) Does the history of convictions establish a propensity to commit offences of the kind charged?

   (ii) Does the propensity make it more likely that the defendant committed the offence charged?

   (iii) Would it be unjust to rely on convictions of the same description or category; and would the proceedings be unfair if those convictions were admitted?

6. Note that s103(2) merely provides examples of how propensity to commit offences of the kind charged may be proved. In *R v Weir* (2005), W was convicted of a sexual assault on a 10-year-old girl. Evidence was admitted that W had been cautioned in August 2000 for taking an indecent photograph of a child. That offence was neither of the same description or of the same category as the offence for which he was charged. The Court of Appeal held the trial judge had been right to admit the caution as evidence of propensity under s101(1)(d). In *R v Chopra* (2007), Hughes LJ held that the 'evidence of several complainants is cross-admissible if, but only if, it is relevant to an important matter in issue between the defendant and the prosecution'. The defendant was charged with several similar counts of indecently assaulting young female patients during the course of medical examination. Evidence suggesting the defendant committed one count was, so far as one of the other counts was concerned, bad character evidence under CJA 2003 and amounted to propensity.

7. In *R v H* (1995), the defendant was convicted of gross indecency with two stepdaughters. One stepdaughter complained three years after the alleged abuse ceased. When questioned by her mother, the other stepdaughter denied abuse, but having spoken to her sister made similar allegations. The issue of collusion arose and this may be particularly relevant in cases where cross-admissibility is in issue. The House of Lords held in this case that collusion does not affect the admissibility of evidence, only its weight.

8. In *R v Hanson, Gilmour and Pickstone* (2005) the Court of Appeal emphasised that as a general rule, the fewer the previous convictions, the less likely that propensity will be established. A single conviction of the same description or category will often not show propensity; in

other cases, a single conviction committed using an identical *modus operandi* may be highly relevant to establishing both propensity and the probative value of previous convictions.

- In *R v Woodhouse* (2009) the appellant appealed against his conviction for sexual activity with a child. It was held by the Court of Appeal that a single previous incident, which resulted in a caution 10 years previously, was admissible as bad character because the circumstances were so similar.
- In *R v Cundell* (2009) C was charged with soliciting another to murder his former wife. At the time he was serving a term of 5 years' imprisonment, having pleaded guilty to a previous offence of soliciting his wife's murder. Despite being a single previous conviction, it clearly demonstrated propensity.!
- In *R v Urushadze* (2008) Tthe Court of Appeal held that the appellant's six previous convictions for shoplifting were not relevant to show the relevant propensity for robbery.

9. Note the evidence of bad character must be directed at specific issues in the case and not the general propensity of the accused to behave in a particular way.

- In *R v Bullen* (2008) the defendant was convicted of murder. Seven previous convictions for offences of violence were admitted at his trial even though he offered a plea of guilty to manslaughter. The previous convictions related to crimes of basic intent and were not relevant to the key issue of whether the defendant possessed the required specific intention to kill or cause grievous bodily harm and should have been excluded.
- In *R v Tully and Wood* (2007), the trial judge's admission of dishonesty convictions at the defendants' trial for robbery to 'show a propensity to obtain other people's property by one means or another' stretched the concept of 'propensity' too far.

10. Section 103(1)(b) admits evidence of a 'propensity to be untruthful' providing the suggestion relates to untruthfulness in the present trial. The Explanatory Notes to the Act suggest that the sort of evidence envisaged for admission within this section would be convictions for perjury or deception, but there is nothing within the Act to restrict the admission of such evidence in that way. Cases decided since enactment of CJA 2003 indicate 'propensity to be untruthful' will only be an important matter in issue between the prosecution and defence where 'telling lies' is part of the offence itself (see *R v Hanson, Gilmour and Pickstone* (2005) and *R v Campbell* (2007)).

7.5.3 Section 101(1)(e): Important matter in issue between defendant and co-defendant

1. Evidence of bad character is admissible where 'it has substantial probative value in relation to an important matter in issue between the defendant and a co-defendant'. Section 101(1)(e) is only available to a co-defendant and not the prosecution.

2. Inclusion of 'substantial probative value' makes it more difficult for a co-accused to admit evidence of a defendant's previous convictions than for the prosecution under s101(1)(d) and indicates the nature of the difference between the defendants must be substantial.

3. Section 101(1)(e) may admit evidence relevant to (a) propensity and (b) credibility (see *R v Randall* (2004) and *R v De Vos* (2006)). For example:
   (a) Where two or more defendants run cut-throat defences, an important matter in issue between those two defendants will be which of them was more likely to have committed the offence. Bad character evidence may have substantial probative value in relation to that issue. In *R v Musone* (2007) it was held that the appellant's confession to a murder for which he had previously been tried and acquitted could, in theory, be used as evidence of bad character, demonstrating it was more likely that the appellant had stabbed the victim than his co-accused.
   (b) Where defendant 1 (D1) undermines the defence of defendant 2 (D2) (s104(1) CJA 2003) and the bad character evidence has substantial probative value in relation to D1's truthfulness, then bad character evidence can be admitted to show D1's propensity to be untruthful (see *R v Lawson* (2006)).

7.5.4 Section 101(1)(f): Creating a false impression

1. Section 101(1)(f) admits evidence of bad character where the defendant has created a false impression. The gateway is only available to the prosecution. Section 105(1) provides clarification by setting out the circumstances in which bad character evidence will be admitted:
   '(a) the defendant gives a false impression if he is responsible for the making of an express or implied assertion which is apt to give the court or jury a false or misleading impression about the defendant;
   (b) the evidence to correct such an impression is evidence which has probative value in correcting it'.

2. The defendant can create a false impression through express and implied assertions. In *R v Ullah* (2006) the appellant's express assertion that he ran a reputable company and had never acted dishonestly at his trial for conspiracy to defraud, triggered gateway s101(1)(f) and his previous conviction for obtaining property by deception was admissible.

3. An accused may create a false impression through his own testimony, through responses to questioning at the police station or through cross-examination of witnesses at trial (see s.105(2)).
   In *R v Renda* (2005) the appellant had given evidence in chief designed to create a false impression and thus enhance his credibility. During cross-examination he conceded that this evidence was false. Section 105(3) lays down that where a defendant withdraws a false impression or disassociates himself from it, it is no longer appropriate to treat him as having created a false impression. The Court of Appeal in *Renda* held that a concession extracted from a defendant under cross-examination is not a withdrawal or disassociation under s105(3). In those circumstances it is right that the defendant should be cross-examined on bad character.

4. Under s105(4) CJA 2003 a false impression may also be created by a defendant through his conduct in the proceedings. Section. 105(5) confirms such 'conduct' includes appearance or dress. Potentially this might have broadened the previous law by allowing the admission of a defendant's convictions should his choice of clothing at trial suggest he is of good character (the obvious example would be the wearing of a clerical collar to suggest employment by the Church (see *R v Hamilton* (1979) for an example of the previous position).

5. In another sense, s101(1)(f) restricts the admission of previous convictions by allowing evidence 'only if it goes no further than is necessary to correct the false impression' (s105(6)). Under the previous law an assertion of good character would trigger cross-examination on all aspects of the defendant's bad character. Under s101(1)(f) the prosecutor will be restricted to the admission of such part of the defendant's previous convictions as is necessary to correct the false impression.

6. A concern about s101(1)(f) is that the gateway may be triggered by an over-enthusiastic denial of guilt during police questioning.
   The Court of Appeal in *R v Somanathan* (2005) expressed the view that s78 PACE 1984 should be considered when admitting evidence of bad character under s101(1)(f).

7.5.5 Section 101(1)(g): Making an attack on another person's character

1. Section 101(1)(g) allows for the admission of evidence of bad character where a defendant 'has made an attack on another person's character'. Whilst the previous law allowed the admission of previous convictions only where imputations were made against the prosecutor, a prosecution witness or the dead victim of an offence, s101(1)(g) admits bad character evidence where an attack is made on any person.

2. A suggestion that a third party, rather than the defendant, might have committed the offence charged is likely to trigger this gateway, as will a suggestion that the other person behaved, or is disposed to behave, in a reprehensible way (s106(2)).

3. Like gateway (f) the attack may be made by the accused in the course of testimony, by a legal adviser during cross-examination, or pre-trial during police interviews (s106(1)). Unlike gateway (f), once triggered, gateway (g) potentially admits the whole of the defendant's bad character evidence.

   In *R v Ball* (2005) the appellant, B, was convicted of rape. The complainant claimed that after intercourse, B asked, 'What are you going to do now, go off and get me done for rape? Look at you, you're nowt but a slag'. During police interviews, B, claimed the complainant had consented and had made a false allegation, motivated by a wish for vengeance. He added: 'She's a bag really, you know what I mean, a slag'. That comment was admitted as part of the prosecution case because B had described the complainant in the same disparaging terms as she alleged he had used at the time. The trial judge considered exclusion under s101(1)(3) but decided to admit it, and that decision, and B's conviction, were upheld by the Court of Appeal.

4. Much of the pre-CJA 2003 case law remains relevant and it is likely that an accusation that a witness has lied (*R v Britzman and Hall* (1983)) or that a witness has behaved immorally (*Selvey v DPP* (1970)) will be sufficient to trigger the gateway; a robust denial of guilt, supported by a suggestion that a witness is mistaken, will not. In *R v Williams* (2007) the appellant's assertion that the police had colluded together and fabricated evidence against him went so far beyond the criticisms of the police made in his defence statement, that all of his bad character, which included offences of dishonesty, was admissible.

5. The first opportunity for the Court of Appeal to interpret s101(1)
   (g) came with *R v Highton* (2005). H appealed against his conviction
   for kidnapping, robbery and theft on the grounds that although his
   previous convictions were admissible under s101(1)(g), the trial judge
   had misdirected the jury that his bad character was admissible to
   propensity as well as to credibility. The Court of Appeal held that there
   is a distinction between **admissibility** of bad character (which requires
   getting it through one of the gateways) and the **use to which it is put**
   once admitted. Use depends on the matters to which the evidence
   is relevant rather than the gateway through which it is admitted.
   Evidence admitted under s101(1)(g) may be relevant to propensity as
   well +as credibility. This appellant's convictions for offences of violence
   and possession of offensive weapons were relevant to propensity. In *R
   v Lamaletie and Royce* (2008) a list of the defendant's six previous
   convictions for violent offences was admissible under s101(1)(g), at
   his trial for GBH, to show his character in a 'broad, general sense'. The
   fact that it incidentally demonstrated a propensity to commit violent
   offences did not rule it inadmissible.

7.5.6 Safety principles

1. Section 101(1)(3) provides a discretion to exclude evidence under
   s101(1)(d) or (g) where its admission would have such an adverse
   effect on the fairness of the proceedings that the court ought not to
   admit it. Note this discretion does not apply to other gateways. The
   impact admission of bad character evidence will have on the length
   and complexity of proceedings is a factor for the trial judge to take into
   consideration (*R v O'Dowd* (2009)).

2. Students will have noted the similarity in wording between s101(3)
   and s78 PACE 1984, the only difference being that under s101(3) the
   court **must** exclude evidence where its admission would have such an
   adverse effect on the fairness of the proceedings that it ought not to be
   admitted. Under s78(1) the court **may** exclude such evidence.

3. In exercising discretion under s101(3), courts must pay regard to the
   time interval between the matters to which the evidence relates and
   matters which form the subject of the offence charged (s101(4)).

4. The s101(3) discretion is triggered by an application from the defence
   although a judge should encourage the making of an application where
   appropriate (see *R v Somanathan* (2006)).

5. There is nothing in the CJA 2003 which prevents courts from excluding evidence of bad character admissible under gateways (c) and (f) under s78(1) Police and Criminal Evidence Act 1984, and s101(4) specifically provides that 'nothing in the Act affects the exclusion of evidence on grounds other than the fact that it is evidence of the defendant's bad character'. Note the discretion to exclude evidence in s78(1) PACE 1984 extends only to evidence on which the prosecution intends to rely and therefore will not cover gateway (e).

6. Section 107 CJA 2003 stipulates that judges in trials on indictment must stop the case where:
   - evidence is contaminated; and
   - having regard to the importance of the contaminated evidence, the conviction would be unsafe.

7. Courts must give reasons for any character rulings (s110 CJA 2003).

8. The Court of Appeal stressed in *R v Hanson, Pickstone and Gilmour* (2005) that applications to adduce bad character evidence should not be made routinely, but should be carefully balanced according to the facts of the case. The court advised that where the prosecution's case is weak it may be unfair to bolster that evidence by admitting previous convictions, and that the fairness of the proceedings may be adversely affected where convictions are old. Courts should consider each conviction individually rather than automatically admitting all previous convictions where one of the gateways is triggered.

9. The court in *Hanson* stated that the prosecution must indicate at the time of making an application to admit bad character evidence whether they seek to rely merely upon the fact of the conviction or whether they seek to admit evidence relating to the circumstances of the previous offence.

10. Finally, in *Hanson*, the Court of Appeal advised judges upon the terms in which jurors should be directed on bad character:
    - that they should not conclude that a defendant is guilty or untruthful merely because he has convictions;
    - the fact that convictions might show propensity does not inevitably mean that the defendant committed this offence or has been untruthful in this case;
    - that whether convictions in fact show a propensity is for the jury to decide;
    - that they must take into account what a defendant has said about his previous convictions; and

- that, although they are entitled, if they find propensity is shown, to take this into account when determining guilt, propensity is only one relevant factor and they must assess its significance in the light of all the other evidence in the case.

7.6 Other statutory provisions admitting bad character evidence in criminal proceedings

1. Under s27(3) Theft Act 1968 the prosecution may admit evidence of previous misconduct on a charge of handling stolen goods for the purpose of proving that the accused knew or believed the goods were stolen. The section allows for the admission of:
   - evidence that the accused was in possession of or handled stolen goods in the twelve months prior to the current charge; or
   - a conviction for theft or handling within five years preceding the date of the offence charged.
2. A further theoretical statutory exception arises by virtue of s1(2) Official Secrets Act 1911 which allows a defendant to be convicted on the basis of 'his known character as proved'. Not surprisingly, this provision has not been used in recent memory.

7.7 Bad character evidence in civil proceedings

1. Evidence of character is admissible if it amounts to a fact in issue, e.g. evidence of a person's reputation in an action in defamation.
2. Convictions of a party to an action are admissible under s2 Civil Evidence Act 1968 where they are relevant to the facts in issue.
3. Witnesses can be cross-examined on previous convictions under s6 CPA 1865.

7.7.1 Similar fact evidence in civil proceedings

1. In criminal cases prior to the coming into force of CJA 2003 the admission of bad character under similar fact evidence rules was admitted only exceptionally because of the obvious potential for

prejudice leading to wrongful convictions. In civil cases the need for caution is less, and parties are frequently allowed to admit evidence under similar fact evidence rules.

2. Evidence of misconduct on a previous occasion was regarded as admissible according to the Court of Appeal in *Mood Publishing Co Ltd v de Wolfe Publishing Ltd* (1976) providing it was logically probative of a fact in issue and the evidence was neither oppressive nor unfair to the other party.

3. In *O'Brien v Chief Constable of South Wales Police* (2004) these long-established principles were reviewed and dismissed by the Court of Appeal as inappropriate in the light of the civil justice reforms. What is demanded today is a 'cards on the table' approach through the pre-trial exchange of evidence. Brooke LJ described the modern approach to the admission of similar fact evidence as follows:

   ■ 'In deciding how to exercise its discretion, the matters listed in CPR 1(2) must loom large in the court's deliberations. In principle, the stronger the probative force of the similar fact evidence, the more willing the court should be not to exclude it, everything else being equal. On the other hand, the court should have a tendency to refuse to allow similar fact evidence to be called if it would lengthen the proceedings and add to their cost and complexity unless there are strong countervailing arguments the other way'.

Hearsay: the rule, exceptions under the civil evidence act 1995 and at common law

8.1 The hearsay rule

Hearsay evidence is most easily understood by adopting a two-stage approach.

■ Stage one involves the recognition of a statement as hearsay.
■ Stage two requires a consideration of admissibility: a hearsay statement will be admissible in a criminal trial only if the statement falls within a common law exception to the hearsay rule (see 8.3) or under the CJA 2003 (see Chapter 9).

TEST FOR RECOGNISING A HEARSAY STATEMENT

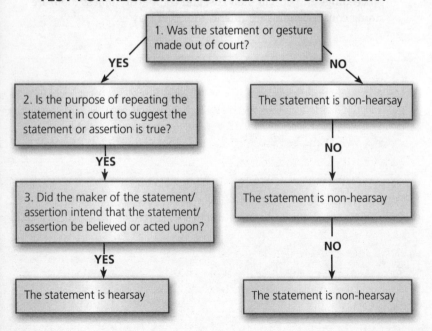

8.1.1 Hearsay evidence: exclusionary or inclusionary?

The wording of the CJA 2003 suggests an inclusionary approach to hearsay: instead of stating that 'hearsay evidence is inadmissible unless …', the Act states that a 'hearsay statement is admissible, but only if …'. The change in terminology has made hearsay statements in criminal trials more readily admissible, yet it remains necessary to identify the section of the Act or common law rule that permits the admission of a particular hearsay statement. On that basis the rule remains exclusionary, but subject to a wide range of exceptions.

In civil proceedings the modern rule is inclusionary: hearsay is always admissible subject to safeguards.

8.1.2 Defining and recognising hearsay

1. Cross defined the rule as: *an assertion other than one made by a person while giving oral evidence in the proceedings is inadmissible as evidence of any fact stated.* More useful to students in identifying a hearsay statement is to apply the three-pronged test in diagrammatic form at 8.1. Put another way, hearsay is:

   (a) anything said or written outside the courtroom **if**
   (b) it is being used to prove the truth of what is contained in those words or writing, **and if**
   (c) the intention of the maker was that the words should be believed or acted upon.

Example 1

D is charged with murdering V, an act witnessed by W. W could plainly give original evidence of what he saw. Suppose W tells a third party, X, that he saw D murder V, before he, W suffers a complete mental break-down. Can X attend court and tell the jury what W told him he had seen?

Applying the three questions:

(1) The statement from W to X was made out of court.

(2) The purpose of repeating W's statement in court would be to suggest that the words used were true and that D did indeed murder V.

(3) W intended X to believe his assertion.

Since the answer to all three questions is 'Yes', the statement is hearsay. Had any of the answers been 'No' the statement would be non-hearsay.

Example 2

Suppose that D is in fact innocent. Instead of D being charged with murder, D brings an action in defamation against W. Would X be allowed to testify as to what D told him?

Applying the questions:

(1) The statement from W to X was made out of court;

(2) The intention of W was that his statement should be believed by X;

(3) But in this scenario, the purpose of repeating W's statement in court is not to prove that W's words were true, simply that the statement was made. The answer to that question being 'No', W's statement is non-hearsay.

2. The standard textbook definition of hearsay derives from *Subramaniam v Public Prosecutor* (1956). Subramaniam (S) was charged with unlawful possession of ammunition under emergency regulations. It was a defence to the charge to have lawful excuse for the possession, and S sought to testify that he had been captured by terrorists and acted under duress. The trial judge ruled he could not state in evidence what the terrorists said to him. The Privy Council held that such evidence was admissible since the object of such evidence was not to establish the truth of what the terrorists said to him, but merely the fact that the statement was made and the effect of the threat upon the defendant.

8.1.3 Scope of the hearsay rule

1. The exclusionary rule has traditionally been more stringently applied in criminal than in civil cases (see *R v McLean* (1967)).

2. The hearsay rule applies equally to statements made orally (*R v Teper* (1952)), in writing (*R v Lydon* (1986)), or by means of gestures (*R v Gibson* (1887)).

3. Whilst the rule is justified on the grounds that hearsay evidence is potentially unreliable, and because of the impossibility of cross-examining on hearsay evidence, the cases of *Sparks v R* (1964) and *R v Turner* (1975)) illustrate that the rule can disadvantage defendants as well as prosecutors.

4. The House of Lords in *R v Kearley* (1992) recognised a further form of hearsay evidence: the implied assertion.

- The House of Lords by a 3:2 majority found that evidence of what was said by several different people, both on the telephone and in person, indicating that they wished to purchase drugs, was hearsay and inadmissible. The purpose of repeating the words used by the callers was not to prove merely that the words were spoken, but to show that the callers believed Kearley was involved in the supply of drugs and were correct in that assumption. On that basis the words were hearsay.
- As a result of the third part of the reformed test for hearsay under s115(3), implied assertions no longer fall within the rule. Such assertions will in future be admissible as non-hearsay subject only to the test of relevance.

8.2 Exceptions to the hearsay rule in civil cases: the Civil Evidence Act 1995

1. One of the principal reasons for the development of the hearsay rule was because of the involvement of lay persons, particularly lay jurors in the trial process.

2. One of the principal reasons for the decline of the rule in civil proceedings was because of the decline in the involvement of lay persons.

3. Judges, it is felt, are capable of appreciating that evidence varies in terms of quality and reliability. Evidence which lacks reliability will be accorded less weight by professional judges.

4. The Civil Evidence Acts 1968 and 1972 were important steps towards admitting hearsay statements in civil proceedings more liberally, but the Acts were unnecessarily complex and many believed they did not go far enough.

5. The CEA 1995 repealed Part I of the 1968 Act and simplified the rules considerably; the new Act was based upon the principle that hearsay evidence should be admissible in civil proceedings, but subject to certain safeguards.

6. Procedural matters are dealt with by the Civil Procedure Rules (CPR 33).

8.2.1 The substance of the Civil Evidence Act 1995

1. Section 1(1) of the CEA 1995 states that 'In civil proceedings evidence shall not be excluded on the ground that it is hearsay. The effect of this is to make all hearsay statements admissible in civil proceedings – an inclusionary rule.

2. Section 1(2)(a) adopts the standard common law definition of hearsay.

3. Section 1(2)(b) makes clear that all hearsay evidence is admissible whether it is first-hand, second-hand or has passed through multiple hands.

4. A 'statement' is defined in s13 as 'any representation of fact or opinion however made'. The term includes written statements, oral statements and gestures, and under the Civil Evidence Act 1972, statements of opinion.

5. Where a party seeks to introduce evidence that is admissible in its own right, the CEA 1995 will not apply (s1(3) and (4)). An example of evidence admissible in its own right would be a statement admitted under ss3–6 of the Criminal Procedure Act 1865 which is used to discredit a hostile witness. Because such a statement is admissible without recourse to the CEA 1995, the safeguards, including the Notice Procedure, imposed by s2 of the CEA 1995 do not apply.

8.2.2 Safeguards under the CEA 1995

Section 2 of the CEA 1995 lays down safeguards that are designed to counter the potential unreliability of hearsay evidence.

1. Subsection (1) deals with the requirement upon the party adducing the hearsay evidence to notify other parties of the intention to do so and to provide details of that evidence. This ensures that other parties in the proceedings are not taken by surprise, and gives them the opportunity, if it is practicable, to insist upon the attendance of a witness.

2. Time limits for the serving of notice are laid down by CPR rule 33.2(4)(a). Failure to serve notice in accordance with rule 33.2.4(a) does not affect the admissibility of the statement but will affect the weight accorded to the statement (s2(4) CEA 1995) or result in an adjournment (s2(4)(b)).

3. The notice procedure can be waived by agreement between the parties (s2(3)).

4. Where hearsay evidence is adduced at trial, it is open to other parties under s5(2) of the CEA 1995 to attack the credibility of the hearsay witness by demonstrating that the witness has made another contradictory statement. This can be done by producing any evidence which would have been admissible had the hearsay witness testified in person.

5. Section 5(2) is designed to counter the disadvantage of being unable to cross-examine on a hearsay statement and to enable the judge to form a view about the weight that can properly be accorded to the hearsay statement.

6. Where a party wishes to make use of s5(2) that party must serve notice of his intention upon the party proposing to adduce the hearsay statement.

8.2.3 Weight attaching to hearsay statements under the CEA 1995

1. Section 2(4) of the CEA 1995 places responsibility for assessing the quality of hearsay evidence with the trial judge.

2. In deciding how much weight to accord to hearsay statements, the judge is obliged to consider all those circumstances that might affect the reliability of the evidence.

3. Listed in s4(2) of the Act are guidelines to assist judges rather than hard and fast rules.

4. An overview of the factors which judges should consider makes it clear that hearsay evidence continues to be regarded with some scepticism.

5. Section 4(2)(a) advises judges to consider the reasons why a party has chosen to adduce hearsay evidence in preference to calling the witness. If there is no valid reason for relying upon hearsay evidence instead of calling the witness, then little weight will be given to that evidence.

6. In *Clingham v Kensington and Chelsea RLBC* (2002), C appealed against an anti-social behaviour order granted to the local council following admission of anonymous evidence. C contended that he was denied the right to cross-examine the witness which breached his right to a fair trial under Article 6 ECHR. In dismissing the appeal the court confirmed that applications for anti-social behaviour orders are civil proceedings and the admission of hearsay evidence is governed by CEA 1995. On that basis, it was for the magistrates' court to decide the weight to attach to it pursuant to s4(2) of the Act.

7. Even where hearsay evidence is the only evidence on which a claim is based, this will not necessarily provide a reason for giving it no weight. In *Welsh v Stokes* (2008) the Court of Appeal upheld a decision to rely on such hearsay evidence where the trial judge had given proper regard to the factors in s4s4(2).

8.2.4 Supplementary matters

1. Section 6 deals with previous statements of witnesses. The CEA 1995 does not merely apply to the statements of witnesses who are not called to give evidence in person; it applies equally to a previous statement made by a person who gives oral testimony where that witness has also made a written or oral statement previously.

2. Subsection (2) goes on to say that a party who intends to call a person as a witness may not adduce evidence of a previous statement except with leave of the court or for the purpose of rebutting a suggestion that his evidence has been fabricated.

3. Section 7 deals with common law exceptions to the hearsay rule, retaining those previously preserved by s9 Civil Evidence Act 1968, i.e.
   - published works and public documents;
   - records;
   - evidence of a person's reputation for the purpose of proving good or bad character;
   - evidence of reputation or family tradition for the purpose of proving or disproving pedigree or the existence of a marriage, or the existence of a public or general right or the identification or any person or thing.

Where a statement is admissible under a common law exception to the rule against hearsay there is no need for the party seeking to adduce the statement to follow the procedures and safeguards contained in s2 and 6 of the CEA 1995.

8.2.5 Overview of the Civil Evidence Act 1995

1. In civil proceedings, evidence shall not be excluded on the ground that it is hearsay.

2. Unless the parties agree otherwise, a party proposing to adduce hearsay evidence in civil proceedings must serve notice on the other party/ies and, on request, such particulars as are reasonable and

practicable in order to allow him to deal with any matters arising from the hearsay evidence.

3. In assessing the weight to be given to hearsay evidence in civil proceedings, the court shall have regard to any circumstances from which inferences can reasonably be drawn as to the reliability or otherwise of the evidence.

4. The CEA 1995 does not abolish the common law exceptions to the hearsay rule, though it does supersede the exception covering informal admissions.

8.3 Common law exceptions to the hearsay rule in criminal cases

Section 114(1)(b) CJA 2003 expressly preserves a number of common law exceptions to the hearsay rule contained within s118. Those not included within s118 are abolished by the Act. Admissible under s118(1) as evidence of the facts stated are documents that contain:

1. Public information etc. This exception includes:
   (a) published works dealing with matters of a public nature (such as histories, scientific works, dictionaries and maps);
   (b) public documents (such as public registers);
   (c) records (such as court records, treaties etc.);
   (d) evidence relating to a person's age or date or place of birth. This evidence may be given by a person without personal knowledge of the matter.
   ■ This collection of common law exceptions is self-explanatory. Many documents of a public nature will also be admissible in criminal proceedings under s117 CJA 2003 (see Chapter 9).

2. Reputation as to character: this has long been problematic at common law, and the preservation of this exception, without clarification, has done little to resolve the difficulties. In *Rowton* (1865–73) it was held that although evidence of general reputation is admissible, evidence of specific acts and deeds is not. *Rowton* has not always been rigorously followed.

3. Reputation or family tradition. This covers:
   (a) pedigree or the existence of a marriage;
   (b) the existence of any public or general right; or
   (c) the identity of any person or thing.

4. *Res gestae* (this important and versatile exception is dealt with fully at 8.4).

5. Confessions etc. These are regulated, in the main, by s76 PACE 1984, which is fully examined in Chapter 10. Evidence of implied admissions are admissible at common law. This would include the defendant's reaction to a charge or allegation when first accused, particularly where his reaction suggests acceptance of the allegation in circumstances where a denial might be expected from an innocent person.

6. Admissions by agents etc.

7. Common enterprise.

8. Expert evidence: s118(1) preserves the common law rule under which, in criminal proceedings, an expert witness may draw on the body of expertise relevant to his field (see Chapter 12).

Any common law exceptions not included within that list are abolished by s118(2). The most important of those exceptions not retained is dying declarations. Although abolished by the Act, most dying declarations will remain admissible in criminal trials under s116 or as part of the *res gestae*. Also abolished are declarations against interest and declarations in the course of duty made by persons since deceased. Again, evidence previously admissible at common law may be admissible under s116 or s117 CJA 2003.

8.4 *Res gestae*

1. *Res gestae* (literally 'things done') is the most important of the surviving common law exceptions, which allows the admission of hearsay evidence to explain some contemporaneous act or state of affairs.

2. The pre-CJA case law on *res gestae* remains relevant since ss114(1)(d) and 118(1)(4) simply preserve the common law exception without alteration. Note that some hearsay statements admissible as part of the *res gestae* may also be admissible under s116 CJA 2003.

8.4.1 Statements explaining actions (s118(1)(4)(b) CJA 2003)

A statement by an actor may be the best means of explaining the significance of the act where that is relevant to an issue (see *The Aylesford Peerage Case* (1885)). To be admissible as *res gestae* the statement must:

- relate directly to the act;
- have been made contemporaneously with the act;
- be made by the actor.

8.4.2 Statements as to physical or mental condition (s118(1)(4)(c) CJA 2003)

- Statements relating to the contemporaneous physical or mental condition, including the emotions, of the speaker, are admissible as *res gestae*.
- Although statements as to sensations or symptoms are admissible, the reasons for those sensations or symptoms are inadmissible (*Gilbey v Great Western Railway* (1910)).

8.4.3 Statements of intention (s118(1)(4)(c) CJA 2003)

A statement of intention may be admissible as evidence of that intention, but whether it is also admissible evidence of his acting in accordance with his intention is uncertain.

- In *Wainwright* (1875) V's statement to a friend that she intended to meet her boyfriend on the day of her death was inadmissible at W's trial for murder since there was no evidence that she had carried out her intention.
- In *Buckley* (1873) a police officer's statement to his superior officer that he intended to keep surveillance on B on the night of his murder was admitted at B's trial for murder as evidence of what the officer was doing at the time of his death. The constable, having informed his superior officer of his intentions, was under a duty to act upon those intentions.

8.4.4 Spontaneous statements by actors or observers (s118(1)(4)(a) CJA 2003)

1. Historically, the need for contemporaneity was very strong within this species of *res gestae* (see *R v Bedingfield* (1879) for an example of a case which failed because the statement was not sufficiently contemporaneous).

2. Clarification was achieved in *Ratten v R* (1972) when the Privy Council considered the admissibility of a telephone call to emergency services from a woman shortly before her death. It was held to be non-hearsay, but the Privy Council expressed the view that had the statement been

hearsay, it would have been admissible as *res gestae*. Lord Wilberforce stated: 'There was ample evidence of the close and intimate connection between the statement ascribed to the deceased and the shooting which occurred very shortly afterwards. They were closely associated in place and in time'. This case is seen as illustrative of the move away from a need for strict contemporaneity towards a need for spontaneity brought about by a dramatic event that controls the mind of the speaker.

3. In *R v Andrews* (1987) the House of Lords, overruling *Bedingfield* and approving *Ratten*, laid down guidelines for the admission of *res gestae* statements under this head.

   ■ The trial judge must be satisfied that the possibility of concoction or distortion can be disregarded.

   ■ In deciding whether concoction or distortion can be safely disregarded, the judge must be satisfied that the event was 'so unusual or startling or dramatic as to dominate the thoughts of the victim, so that his utterance was an instinctive reaction to that event'.

   ■ The statement must be closely associated with the event in order to be sufficiently spontaneous for admissibility and the trial judge 'must be satisfied that the event which provided the trigger mechanism for the statement, was still operative. The fact that the statement was made in answer to a question is but one factor to consider ...'.

   ■ The trial judge must be satisfied that the statement was not initiated by malice and that the possibility of error could be ruled out. Once the statement is ruled admissible, the judge must 'make it clear to the jury that it is for them to decide what was said and to be sure that the witnesses were not mistaken in what they believed had been said to them'.

4. An identification of a car driver some 20 minutes after a minor traffic accident was held inadmissible as *res gestae* in *Tobi v Nicholas* (1988) on the ground that there was no evidence of any event of sufficient drama to control or affect his mind.

5. In *Re Attorney General's Reference (No 1 of 2003)* the prosecution sought to present evidence of two witnesses who had seen M, the defendant's mother, lying on the steps of her home in fear and distress. M told the witnesses that her son, W, had thrown her downstairs and set fire to her hair. Her son was charged with causing grievous bodily harm with

intent. M was unwilling to testify against her son and the prosecution sought to admit evidence from the two witnesses as part of the *res gestae*. The Attorney General sought a ruling from the Court of Appeal as to whether such a statement was admissible. The Court of Appeal ruled that the prosecution should not use *res gestae* as a mechanism to avoid calling an available witness, however once evidence is admissible as part of the *res gestae* it must not be excluded purely because the witness was available. Evidence should be excluded under s78(1) PACE 1984 where its admission would have an adverse effect on the fairness of the proceedings. The issue should be dealt with as a matter of discretion rather than law.

9

Statutory exceptions to the hearsay rule in criminal cases

Unavailability exception s116 CJA 2003	Business exception s117 CJA 2003
Admits oral and written statement of properly identified absent witness whose evidence would otherwise have been admissible where witness: • dead; • unfit through bodily or mental condition; • outside UK; • cannot be found; • does not give evidence through fear.	Admits documentary hearsay providing oral evidence of the matters stated would have been admissible and the document is: • created or received in course of business; • from information supplied by person with personal knowledge; • where intermediaries received information in the course of business.

9.1 Introduction

The CJA 2003 has significantly reduced the scope of the hearsay rule. Under s114(1) hearsay statements are admissible as evidence of any matter stated only:

    (a) by statute;

    (b) at common law (under the rules preserved by s118);

    (c) by agreement; or

    (d) in the interests of justice (the 'safety valve').

9.2 Definitions

1. Section 115(2) CJA 2003 defines the term 'statement':

'A statement is any representation of fact or opinion made by a person by whatever means; and it includes a representation made in a sketch, photofit or other pictorial form'.

- In *R v Leonard* (2009) text messages are capable of amounting to hearsay evidence within the meanings of ss 114 and 115 CJA 2003.
- The term 'person' excludes photographs, video recordings and audio tapes, which are produced, not by a person, but by a mechanical process. Such evidence is non-hearsay (*Taylor v Chief Constable of Cheshire* (1987) is given statutory approval).
- Case law such as *R v Smith (Percy)* (1976) and *R v Cook* (1987), which related to a sketch made by a police officer, and a photofit picture compiled from a description by a witness, are effectively overruled by s115(2): those images are now 'statements', and thus hearsay, though normally admissible under the Act.

2. Section 115(3) CJA 2003 defines the term 'matter stated': 'A matter stated is one to which this Chapter applies if (and only if) the purpose, or one of the purposes, of the statement appears to the court to have been (a) to cause another person to believe the matter, or (b) to cause another person to act or a machine to operate on the basis that the matter is as stated'.

- This section, which added a 'third limb' to the test for hearsay (see 8.1), was designed to exclude the implied assertion (see *R v Kearley* (1992)).
- In *R v N* (2006) the appellant appealed against his convictions for indecent assault and sexual intercourse with a girl under 16. N argued his victim's diary entries were hearsay and therefore should have been inadmissible. The Court of Appeal held the diary entries were not hearsay as the victim had never intended they would be read by, or relied upon by others and therefore they did not fall within s115 CJA 2003.

9.3 The safety valve

1. Section 114(1)(d) allows for the admission of hearsay if 'the court is satisfied that it is in the interests of justice for it to be admissible'. The section may be used where a hearsay statement is inadmissible under any other exception.

2. In *R v Marsh* (2008) the Court of Appeal made it clear that the 'interests of justice' do not necessarily mean the interests of the defendant. Hughes LJ said 'they mean the public interest in arriving at the right conclusion in the case.' (see also *R v Sadiq* (2009)).

3. Section 114(2) lists factors that must be considered in deciding whether to admit a statement under the safety valve. These include:
   - the probative value of the evidence;
   - the availability of other evidence relating to the matter;
   - the importance of the evidence in the context of the case as a whole;
   - the circumstances in which the statement was made;
   - the reliability of the maker of the statement;
   - whether oral evidence could be given, and if not, why not;
   - the difficulty in challenging the statement and the extent to which that difficulty might prejudice the party facing it;
   - any other factors that appear relevant.

The list is not intended to be exhaustive and does not require the judge to make a decision on each factor (*R v Taylor* (2006)).

4. The safety valve is available to both prosecution and defence but was designed to be used sparingly, in cases such as *R v Sparks* (1964) and *R v Lawless* (2003) to avoid potential miscarriages of justice. It emerges from the case law, however, that the courts take a more relaxed approach to the admission of evidence under s114 CJA 2003 and the Court of Appeal will only interfere with the decision of a trial judge where it falls outside the range of reasonable decisions available to the judge (see *R v Sadiq* (2009) and *R v Musone* (2007)). The Court of Appeal may intervene where the trial judge has not considered, or not shown that he has considered, the factors in s114(2) CJA 2003 (see *R v Z* (2009)).

5. Section 114(1)(d) is available to all sorts of hearsay evidence and this may include the confession of a co-accused. In *R v Y* (2008) the confession of a co-accused was admissible even though it incriminated the defendant. In *R v L* (2008) the Court of Appeal upheld a conviction where a wife's statement was admitted in evidence against her husband under s114(1)(d) despite her decision not to give evidence and the provisions of s.8s80 PACE 1984 (see 3.2.2).

6. Where a witness is able to give evidence but does not wish to do so, it may be possible to admit the evidence under s114(d) in 'exceptional circumstances', although 'such an approach would not normally be

in the interests of justice'(*R v Sadiq* (2009)). The appellants appealed against their convictions for attempted murder. The victim had been shot and was left paralysed and unable to speak. He gave evidence at trial by pointing at letters on an alphabet board. The jury were unable to reach a verdict and a re-trial took place. The victim refused to give evidence, giving no reason for his decision. The prosecution could not admit his evidence under s116 CJA 2003 but successfully argued for its admission under s114(d) CJA. In *R v Finch* (2007) the Court of Appeal upheld the trial judge's decision not to admit statements of a witness, who was a former co-accused and available to give evidence if compelled to do so, simply because he was reluctant to enter the witness box.

7. In *R v Z* (2009) the trial judge allowed important evidence of two witnesses (one of whom was dead and the other reluctant to give evidence) to be admitted under s114(1)(d). The Court of Appeal made it clear that s.1s114(1)(d) should be used cautiously and could not be used to circumvent s116 CJA 2003 to admit hearsay evidence.

8. In *R v Horncastle and Others* (2009) (*R v Horncastle* (2009)) the court stressed the importance of being able to confront witnesses as a part of a fair trial under Article 6 ECHR and the need to give witnesses all possible support and to make all possible efforts to get them to trial.

9.4 Hearsay admissible by statute

Confessions remain admissible under s76(1) PACE 1984, dealt with fully in Chapter 10. This chapter deals primarily with hearsay admissible under CJA 2003.

9.4.1 The unavailability exception: s116 CJA 2003

1. Section 116(1), known as the unavailability exception, admits oral and written statements of absent witnesses providing three conditions are satisfied:
   (a) the witness' oral evidence would have been admissible had the witness been available;
   (b) the person who made the statement is identified to the court's satisfaction;
   (c) one of the five conditions in subsection (2) is satisfied.

2. The first condition prevents any party from admitting evidence under s116(1) which would otherwise have been inadmissible. In *R v Sparks* (1964) the 3-year-old victim of the indecent assault was incompetent to testify. Her statement could not have been admitted under this section since her oral evidence was inadmissible.

3. The second condition – that the 'relevant person', i.e. the maker of the statement, must be satisfactorily identified – would prevent the admission of the hearsay statement in *R v Teper* (1952). (The person who had suggested the defendant was guilty of arson was an unidentified passer-by.)

4. The third condition is that the reason for unavailability of the 'relevant person' must be one of those specified in subsection (2). The witness must be either:
   (a) dead;
   (b) unfit to give evidence because of his bodily or mental condition;
   (c) outside the United Kingdom and it is not reasonably practicable to secure his attendance;
   (d) the relevant person cannot be found, although such steps as is reasonably practicable to take to find him have been taken;
   (e) through fear the relevant person does not give (or does not continue to give) oral evidence in the proceedings, either at all or in connection with the subject matter of the statement, and the court gives leave for the statement to be given in evidence.

5. These conditions are almost identical to the conditions that had to be satisfied under s23(3) of the Criminal Justice Act 1988 (CJA 1988). The main difference is that under s23 CJA 1988 only statements made in documents were admissible, whilst under s116 first-hand hearsay statements are admissible whether oral or written.

6. The admission of hearsay is automatic where the reason for unavailability is one of those listed in (a) to (d), above. Where the reason for non-attendance is through fear, the statement will be admissible only where the judge is satisfied that its admission is in the interests of justice (s116(4) CJA 2003).

7. Applications to admit evidence under s116 should be accompanied by agreed facts or evidence and should not proceed informally (*R v T (D)* (2009)).

9.4.2 Relevance of previous case law under s116

1. The inclusion of oral statements within s116(1) allows the now obsolete common law exception to the hearsay rule, dying declarations, to be admitted under s116(2)(a).

2. Paragraph (b) is sufficiently wide to allow an application under s116 even where a witness attends trial and begins to testify. In *R v Setz-Dempsey* (1994) a witness statement was admitted when it became clear that the witness was unable to recall facts coherently. In *R (Meredith) v Harwich Justices* (2007) it was held that a statement from a doctor, asserting that it would be in the witness's best interests to submit written evidence, was not sufficient in itself to prove she was unfit to give evidence because of her mental condition.

3. Where a witness is outside the UK a party wishing to rely on his evidence must satisfy the reasonable practicability requirement in (c). Where it would be expensive or impractical to secure the attendance of the witness, the hearsay statement may be admitted. This paragraph is identical to s23(3)(c) CJA 1988 and previous case law remains relevant.

   - In *R v Bray* (1988) the prosecution had discovered the absence of a witness, who was abroad, as the trial began. Had they known of the witness's plans in advance they would have taken steps to ensure his attendance. On those facts the prosecution had failed to prove that it was not reasonably practicable to secure his attendance.

   - In *R v Case* (1991) the prosecution sought to prove that witnesses were outside the UK by reference to their hearsay statements. That was not allowed. The statement is inadmissible until the condition is satisfied, hence the statement itself cannot be used to prove the condition.

   In *R v Castillo* (1996) the Court of Appeal confirmed the importance of the evidence and how prejudicial it is to the defendant are factors that must be considered.

   In *R v C* (2006) the Court of Appeal held that whether it was fair to admit the evidence 'depended in part on what efforts [c]ould reasonably be made' to secure the witness's attendance or to arrange an alternative procedure, e.g. video link.

4. Paragraph (d) admits hearsay evidence where the relevant person cannot be found despite the party wishing to call the witness having taken reasonable steps to find him.

- In *R v Adams* (2008) Hughes LJ criticised the prosecution for making just one telephone call to the witness two months before the trial and then leaving a voicemail message on a mobile telephone on the last working day before the trial. He said 'leaving contact with the witness such as this until the last working day before the trial is not good enough' and that it is certainly not 'such steps as it is reasonably practicable to take to find him'.

5. Paragraph (e) admits hearsay evidence where the absent witness does not give evidence through fear and the court gives leave for the evidence to be admitted. This provision is wider than its predecessor under s23(3) CJA 1988, which admitted such statements only if made to police officers or to others charged with the duty of investigating offences. As a result of paragraph (e), statements of defence witnesses who are in fear or are kept out of the way become admissible, even where these have been made to a solicitor or others rather than a police officer.

- Section 116(3) clarifies 'fear' which is 'to be widely construed and (for example) includes fear of the death or injury of another person or of financial loss'.
- Section 116 does not require the fear to be attributable to overt threats made by the defendant or his associates:, reputation may be enough. A 'climate of fear' in certain communities and geographical areas may also be sufficient (*R v Horncastle* (2009)).
- Witnesses should never be given an assurance that their statements will be read. The most that a witness can be told is that witnesses are expected to be seen in court and any departure from that principle will be exceptional. The decision is a matter for the judge and not the police. In *R v Marquis and Graham* (2009) (in the appeals of *R v Horncastle and Others* (2009)) the police had 'significantly contributed to the fear of the witness'.
- Pre-existing case law on a witness's absence through fear remains relevant. In *Neill v Antrim Magistrates' Court* (1992) the prosecution wanted to admit the written statements of two children who were too frightened to testify. A police officer gave evidence of their fear following a conversation with their mother. It was held by the Court of Appeal that this was unacceptable: the prosecution should have made direct contact with the witnesses to establish their state of mind at the time of trial.

- *In R v H, W and M* (2001) the victim of an offence made a statement to police in which he said he intended to disappear because he feared he would be killed. The trial judge admitted the statement even though nobody connected with this case had made contact with the victim since the making of his statement. As with *R v Case*, it was not appropriate for the prosecution to use a hearsay statement to prove the admissibility of that hearsay statement and the conviction was quashed.
- Where it emerges during the course of testimony that a witness is in fear, the statement may be admitted at that point (*R v Ashford Justices ex parte Hilden* (1993)).
- Note that s116(1)(e) is the only paragraph to which a leave requirement is attached. Under s26 CJA 1988 leave had to be obtained whatever the witness's reason for absence, and leave could only be given where the court believed the admission of the statement was in the interests of justice.
- The criteria for granting leave are established in s116(4). The court must be satisfied that the admission of the statement is in the interests of justice, having regard to:
'(a) the statement's contents;
(b) any risk that its admission or exclusion will result in unfairness to any party to the proceedings (and in particular to how difficult it will be to challenge the statement if the relevant person does not give oral evidence);
(c) in appropriate cases, the fact that a Special Measures direction under s19 of the YJCEA 1999 could be made in relation to the relevant person; and
(d) any other relevant circumstances'.
- Consideration of the factors (a)-(d) above will be an important part of ensuring a fair trial in accordance with Article 6(3) ECHR (see *R v Sellick* (2005) and *R v Horncastle* (2009)). The trial judge will need to balance the risk to the defendant of being unable to challenge the evidence against the unfairness to the prosecution of being unable to introduce it (see *R v Doherty* (2006)).
- Paragraph (c) refers to Special Measures under the YJCEA 1999. Under s17 YJCEA 1999 witnesses are eligible for assistance 'where the quality of their evidence is likely to be diminished by fear or distress', and s19 entitles the court to decide which of the available measures would be likely to improve the quality of the witness's

evidence. The options would include screens, allowing the witness to testify by means of a video-link, or directing that examination-in-chief be pre-recorded on video.

■ Section 116(5) CJA 2003 prevents a party from using a hearsay statement of a witness he has prevented from attending court through intimidation.

9.4.3 The business exception

1. Section 117(1) CJA 2003 admits a statement contained in a document as evidence of any matter stated providing oral evidence on that matter would have been admissible and that the requirements of subsection (2) are satisfied. The requirements of s117(2) are:

   (a) the document or the part containing the statement was created or received by a person in the course of a trade, business, profession or other occupation, or as the holder of a paid or unpaid office;

   (b) the person who supplied the information contained in the statement (the relevant person) had or may reasonably be supposed to have had personal knowledge of the matters dealt with; and

   (c) each person (if any) through whom the information was supplied from the relevant person to the person mentioned in paragraph (a) received the information in the course of a trade, business, profession or other occupation, or as the holder of a paid or unpaid office.

Example

The prosecution wishes to admit a copy of an invoice produced by a garage relating to work completed on a car. The receptionist prepared the invoice from information provided by the service manager. The mechanic who completed the work had supplied the service manager with the relevant information. In this scenario, the mechanic is the 'relevant person', i.e. the person who supplied the information from personal knowledge. The service manager is the intermediary through whom the information passed and he received the information in the course of trade or business. The receptionist created the document in the course of trade or business. The invoice is admissible under s117.

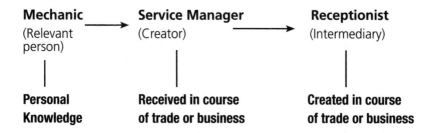

Mechanic	Service Manager	Receptionist
(Relevant person)	(Creator)	(Intermediary)
Personal Knowledge	Received in course of trade or business	Created in course of trade or business

2. Section 117 is similar to s24 CJA 1988 and it is likely that the existence of the required conditions will be inferred from the nature of the document tendered in evidence, as was the position under s24 (see *R v Foxley* (1995)).

3. Under s117(4), where a document is prepared for the purposes of pending or contemplated criminal proceedings, or for a criminal investigation, there must be a statutory reason for non-attendance of the supplier of the information (s117(5)). In addition to the five statutory reasons listed in s116(2), another reason for absence is added: the supplier of the information cannot reasonably be expected to recollect the matters dealt with in the statement, having regard to the length of time since he supplied the information and all other circumstances.

   ■ In *R v Kamuhuza* (2008) the prosecution successfully argued for the admission of written evidence of a police fingerprints officer who had subsequently left the police service and could not be found. The Court of Appeal was not convinced the officer could not be found and rejected the trial judge's view that the evidence could be admitted under s116(2)(d) but was in agreement that the evidence could be admitted under s117(5)(b). It was very unlikely the officer would have been able to recollect any of the forensic evidence some years later.

4. Section 117(7) allows a court to direct that a statement is inadmissible where its reliability is doubtful having regard to:

   (a) its contents;

   (b) the source of the information contained in it;

   (c) the way in which or the circumstances in which the information was supplied or received; or

   (d) the way in which or the circumstances in which the document concerned was created or received.

5. *R v Carrington* (1994) established that parts of a document may be treated as independent statements. In *Carrington*, a statement included a registration number which the witness could not recollect. The part of the statement containing that number was admitted in evidence, even though the witness had no difficulty recollecting the rest of the statement. This case remains relevant under the new regime.

9.5 Safeguards under CJA 2003

1. Section 124 CJA 2003 allows for the admission of relevant evidence relating to the credibility of an absent witness. Under this section, any matter that could have been put to the witness in cross-examination had the witness attended will be admissible, as will evidence of any inconsistent statement made by the witness.

2. Section 125 acknowledges the potential weakness of some hearsay evidence and authorises the court, at any time after the close of the prosecution's case, to direct the acquittal of the defendant or order the discharge of the jury where:
   (a) the case against the defendant is based wholly or partly on a statement not made in oral evidence in the proceedings; and
   (b) the evidence provided by the statement is so unconvincing that, considering its importance to the case against the defendant, his conviction of the offence would be unsafe.

3. The court also has a general discretion, under s126, to exclude hearsay evidence if: 'the court is satisfied that the case for excluding the statement, taking account of the danger that to admit it would result in undue waste of time, substantially outweighs the case for admitting it, taking account of the value of the evidence'.

4. The court has an overriding discretion to exclude any evidence upon which the prosecution proposes to rely under s78(1) PACE 1984.

9.6 Other statutory provisions in criminal proceedings

1. Section 60 of the Youth Justice and Criminal Evidence Act 1999 repeals s69 of PACE 1984 which ceases to have effect. As a result, computerised documentary evidence is now governed by precisely the same rules as any other form of document, namely the person seeking to adduce it

must prove to the requisite standard that:

(a) the document is authentic; and

(b) its contents are admissible.

2. So, if the document contains hearsay, its admission must be secured by bringing it within one of the exceptions to the hearsay rule, for example s117 of the CJA 2003 (see *R v Derodra* (2001), in which a computerised crime report created by a police officer was admissible).

3. Note that with certain types of computer evidence, for example digital cameras, and computerised dialling systems, the computer is regarded as the 'perceiver' and hearsay problems do not arise.

4. Section 30 CJA 1988 admits written reports of expert witnesses, although the leave of the court is required if the expert does not attend (see 12.3.1).

5. Section 9 Criminal Justice Act 1967 applies to criminal proceedings in magistrates' and Crown Courts. It permits the admission of a non-contentious witness statement provided:

(a) it is properly signed;

(b) it contains a declaration as to truth;

(c) a copy is served on other parties;

(d) none of the other parties serve notice objecting to the statement being tendered under s9.

9.7 Human rights implications

1. Whether or not the admission of hearsay evidence breaches the right to a fair trial under Article 6 ECHR, and in particular, the right under Article 6(3)(d) to 'examine or have examined' witnesses who provide evidence as part of the prosecution case at a criminal trial, is still not entirely clear despite the recent decision of the Supreme Court of England and Wales (the Supreme Court) in *R v Horncastle* (2009).

2. A long line of decisions of the European Court of Human Rights (ECtHR) have proved somewhat confusing.

(a) In *Kostovski v The Netherlands* (1990) the ECtHR held that an accused must always be given 'adequate and proper opportunity to challenge and question a witness against him'. This need not necessarily be at trial but at an earlier hearing.

(b) In *Luca v Italy* (2001) the same court decided that 'where a conviction is based solely or to a decisive degree' on evidence the accused has not had the opportunity to challenge, his rights are restricted to an extent that is incompatible with Article 6 ECHR.

(c) In *Al-Khawaja and Tahery v United Kingdom* (2009) the Chamber of the ECtHR followed the 'sole or decisive' reasoning adopted in *Luca* and ruled the appellants' rights under Articles 6(1) and 6(3) (d) had not been respected as the hearsay evidence of dead and fearful witnesses was the 'sole, or at least, the decisive basis' for their conviction. They went on to say that safeguards in CJA 2003 were not sufficient to counterbalance the prejudice caused to the accused. Under Article 43(1) of the ECHR, the United Kingdom requested that the case be referred to the Grand Chamber of the ECtHR for further consideration. The Panel of the Grand Chamber adjourned the case pending the decision of the Supreme Court in *R v Horncastle* (2009). A decision of the Grand Chamber in *Al-Khawaja* remains outstanding.

3. In *R v Horncastle* (2009) the appellants appealed against the use of hearsay evidence admitted under s116(1) and 2(a) CJA 2003 and s116(1) and 2(e) on the basis that it was a decisive element in their convictions, relying on the decision of the ECtHR in *Al-Khawaja*. Both the Court of Appeal and the Supreme Court declined to apply the decision in *Al-Khawaja*. In a hefty unanimous judgment (no doubt designed to persuade the Grand Chamber), Lord Philips set out the following key conclusions of the Supreme Court which can be summarised as follows:

- The common law had addressed the need to ensure a fair trial through the 'hearsay rule' prior to the ECHR coming into force.
- Parliament has enacted a 'regime' under CJA 2003, which provides exceptions to the hearsay rule required in the interests of justice and safeguards that render the 'sole and decisive' rule unnecessary.
- Although the 'sole and decisive rule' is not part of English law, courts would in almost all cases have arrived at the same conclusion as the ECtHR through application of the safeguards in CJA 2003.
- The ECtHR had previously recognised that exceptions to Article 6(3) (d) are required in the interests of justice, e.g. where witnesses are being intimidated (see *Doorson v Netherlands* (1996) and *Grant v The Queen* (2006)).
- The 'sole or decisive' rule does not take into account differences between a common law jurisdiction (where decisions on the rule would need to involve 'mental gymnastics' by a lay -jury) and continental jurisdictions where that decision is made by a professional judge.

In a common law jurisdiction the rule would create significant practical difficulties.

- The case of '*Al-Khawaja* does not establish it is necessary to apply the sole or decisive rule' in England and Wales. Case law of the ECtHR has developed without full consideration of the safeguards against an unfair trial that exist under the common law procedure. The provisions of the CJA 2003 should be interpreted 'in accordance with their natural meaning'.

10

Confessions

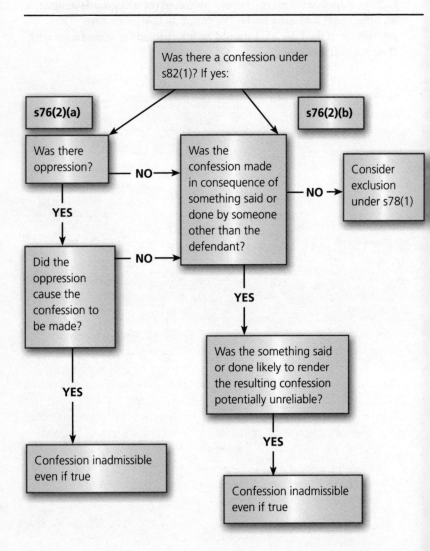

10.1 Introduction

1. An out of court confession will always be hearsay where the purpose of admitting it in evidence is to prove the truth of its contents.

2. Admissibility of confessions is governed by s76 PACE 1984, under which the prosecution has the legal burden of proving that the confession was not obtained by oppression or by anything said or done which might render the confession unreliable.

3. Codes of Practice, created under the authority of PACE, but not part of the Act itself, provide guidance to police officers involved in the detention and interrogation of suspects.

4. Breaches of codes of practice do not render confessions automatically inadmissible, but may make it more difficult for the prosecution to prove admissibility under s76(2). Serious breaches may lead to exclusion of an otherwise admissible confession under s78(1).

10.2 Summary of Code C of Codes of Practice issued under PACE 1984

1. All persons in custody must be dealt with expeditiously, and released as soon as the need for detention has ceased to apply.

2. If an officer has any suspicion that a detained person of any age may be mentally disordered, or is under the age of 17, then he should not be interviewed without the presence of an 'appropriate adult'.
   (a) In the case of juveniles this will normally be a parent or guardian, but may be a social worker or other responsible person over the age of 18.
   (b) In the case of a mentally disordered suspect, a relative, guardian, person experienced in dealing with mental disorders, or some other responsible adult must be present.

3. All persons detained must be informed of their right to receive free legal advice and must not normally (subject to exceptions) be interviewed until legal advice has been received.

4. No police officer should at any time do or say anything with the intention of dissuading a person in detention from obtaining legal advice.

5. Any person detained at a police station who is not under arrest must be informed of his right to leave the police station at any time.

6. Any person arrested and held in custody at a police station is entitled to have one person informed of his whereabouts at public expense.

7. Cells must be adequately heated, cleaned, ventilated and lit, and no additional restraints can normally be used within a locked cell, other than handcuffs where absolutely necessary.

8. Regular meals and drinks must be provided, and, where necessary, advice on diet must be sought from a police doctor.

9. Juveniles must not normally be detained in a cell unless no other secure accommodation is available, and in any event, must not be placed in a cell with a detained adult.

10. A person suspected of having committed an offence must be cautioned before any questions are asked.

11. Where an appropriate adult is present at an interview, he should be informed as to the nature of his role: to advise the person being questioned; to observe whether the interview is being conducted properly and fairly; to facilitate communication.

12. Breaks from interviewing must take place at recognised meal times and short refreshment breaks must normally be provided at approximately two-hourly intervals.

10.3 Definition of confession

1. The partial definition in s82(1) PACE 1984 is that 'confession' includes any statement wholly or partly adverse to the person who made it, whether made to a person in authority or not and whether made in words or otherwise'.

2. A confession can be made orally, in writing or by gesture. In *Li Shu-Ling v R* (1988) the defendant's participation in a re-enactment of the crime was held to be a confession.

3. Statements which are 'wholly or partly adverse' will cover only those that incriminate the maker, or statements those that are 'mixed' and include incriminating and exculpatory elements. Statements that are exculpatory only are not classed as confessions, even if they are used for a different purpose at a later date, e.g an alibi which *was* exculpatory, is shown at trial to be false and therefore has a negative or 'adverse' effect on the defendant's case (see *R v Sat -Bhambra* (1988) and *R v Hasan* (2005)).

10.4 Admissibility under s76

1. A confession is admissible against its maker (and not others) as evidence of the truth of its contents (s76(1)). An exception to this rule was made in *R v Hayter* (2005). H and two co-defendants (B and R) had been charged with murder. B wanted to arrange a contract killing and H recruited R to carry out the killing. Evidence was given at trial of a confession made by R that he had committed the murder. The trial judge directed the jury not to take into account R's confession in the case against H, but told them that if they were satisfied as to the guilt of B and R, they could take that into account, together with other evidence, when considering the case against H. The House of Lords held that this direction was appropriate.

2. In certain circumstances, it may be possible for the prosecution to use a confession against a co-accused under s114(1)(d) CJA 2003 where it is in the interests of justice to do so (see *R v Y* (2008) and at 9.3.5 above).

3. Admissibility may be raised by the defence, or the court itself may, under s76(3), require the prosecution to prove that the confession was not obtained by the methods described in subsection (2).

4. Admissibility will be decided following a *voir dire* and the burden of proof is on the prosecution to prove that the confession is admissible to the standard of 'beyond reasonable doubt'.

5. PACE and the Codes of Practice issued under PACE contain many provisions re arrest, detention, treatment and questioning of suspects. Breach of these rules does not necessarily mean that any resulting confession was obtained by the methods in subsection (2), but MAY do so either alone or with other evidence, or may result in the exclusion of the confession in the exercise of the court's discretion under s78(1).

10.4.1 Oppression under s76(2)(a)

1. Where the prosecution is unable to prove that a confession was not obtained by oppression (s76(2)(a)), the confession will be inadmissible, whether or not it is also considered unreliable.

2. It is only inadmissible where it is made as a result of oppression, so if the confession is made **before** any oppressive conduct, it will be admissible.

3. Section 76(8) defines oppression as 'including torture, inhuman or degrading treatment, and the use or threat of violence (whether or not amounting to torture)'. However, this statutory definition is not used in practice. Instead, the Court of Appeal preferred the ordinary dictionary definition of oppression in *R v Fulling* (1987): 'the exercise of authority or power in a burdensome, harsh or wrongful manner, unjust or cruel treatment of subjects, inferiors etc; the imposition of unreasonable or unjust burdens'.

4. *R v Beales* (1991) and *R v Glaves* (1993) provide examples of oppressive conduct leading to the exclusion of confessions. In *Beales* the court found that the defendant had been 'hectored and bullied from first to last'. In *Glaves* the defendant, aged 16, was subjected to an oppressive interview without an appropriate adult being present.

5. Perhaps the most worrying example of oppressive interrogation techniques is provided by *R v Paris, Abdullahi and Miller* (1993): interviews were held over five days and lasted some 13 hours. The suspect in question had an IQ of 75, just on the borderline of mental handicap. Lord Taylor CJ said:

   'Having denied involvement well over 300 times, he was finally persuaded to make admissions ... [He] was bullied and hectored. The officers ... were not questioning him so much as shouting at him what they wanted him to say. Short of physical violence, it is hard to conceive of a more hostile and intimidating approach by officers to a suspect'.

6. Few confessions will be declared inadmissible under s76(2)(a), and as the cases above illustrate, only where interrogation techniques cross the boundaries of police propriety.

7. *R v Miller* (1986) quite clearly demonstrates that s76(2) is concerned with technical admissibility, not weight or credibility of confessions: the appellant was a paranoid schizophrenic who had confessed to murder. Parts of the confession were consistent with known facts whilst other parts were pure fantasy. It was held that the fact the police interviews might unintentionally have caused hallucinations was not oppression. The confession was admissible. Had officers deliberately set out to produce hallucinations, that would have been oppressive.

8. Conduct which has been held to fall short of oppression includes loss of patience and bad language on the part of a police officer (*R v Emmerson* (1990)) and uncomfortable, cold conditions accompanied by a minor breach of the Code of Practice (*R v Hughes* (1988)).

9. In *R v Mushtaq* (2005) the House of Lords ruled that once a trial judge rules that a confession is admissible under s76(2) a jury is entitled to take that confession into account even where they considered that it might have been obtained by oppression or other improper means.

10.4.2 Unreliability under s76(2)(b)

'Unreliability' must also be given its ordinary dictionary definition: 'cannot be relied upon, untrustworthy or unsafe'.

1. Judges must adopt a subjective approach, taking on board the characteristics of the accused in deciding whether a confession is unreliable.

2. Judges must assess the **potential** unreliability of the confession, not its **actual** unreliability. It would not therefore be appropriate for a judge to consider the truth of a confession in deciding admissibility under s76(2)(b) (see *R v McGovern* (1991)).

3. Unreliability does not require police impropriety (see *R v Sat-Bhambra* (1988)). At the same time, 'things said or done' may be illegal, or in breach of the Act yet not render the confession unreliable where, for example, the accused is an experienced professional criminal (*R v Alladice* (1988)).

4. An example of a confession being excluded under s76(2)(b) is *R v Harvey* (1988). A woman with low intelligence, and who was suffering from a psychopathic disorder, confessed when told by police officers that her lover had confessed. Although there was nothing improper in the conduct of the interview, the Court of Appeal held that the confession might have been a childlike attempt to protect her lover, and was therefore potentially unreliable.

5. Interviewing a juvenile or a person suffering from a mental disorder in the absence of an appropriate adult, or refusing access to legal advice, may be construed as the 'something said or done' which renders a confession unreliable (see *R v Morse and Others* (1991); *R v Blake* (1989); *R v McGovern* (1991).

6. More confessions are declared inadmissible for unreliability under s76(2)(b) than for oppression under s76(2)(a), nevertheless, it should be noted that the statutory test is strictly applied.

7. The cases of *R v Goldenburg* (1988) and *R v Crampton* (1991), where each of the two defendants was a heroin addict, suffering withdrawal at the

time of making his confession, illustrate that courts will not declare confessions inadmissible under s76(2)(b) purely because they are potentially unreliable: such confessions must be unreliable 'in consequence of anything said or done' by a third party.

8. In *R v Blackburn* (2005) the 14-year-old defendant was interviewed at his approved school in the presence of a house warden, but in the absence of his social worker or a solicitor, on suspicion of attempted murder and related offences. The disputed confession originated after over three hours of questioning and a linguistics expert testified that there had been considerable police involvement in that confession. The Court of Appeal held that the statement was inadmissible under s76(2)(b).

10.5 Discretion to exclude an otherwise admissible confession at common law and under s78(1)

Confession evidence can be excluded either at common law or under s78(1) PACE 1984.

10.5.1 Discretion at common law

1. Section 82(3) states: 'Nothing in this part of this Act shall prejudice any power of a court to exclude evidence (whether by preventing questions from being put or otherwise) at its discretion'.

2. This section preserves the common law power of a judge to exclude confession evidence, although the more recent statutory power under s78 is preferred today.

3. Common law powers to exclude confessions were used prior to PACE in three situations:
   (a) where the probative value of the confession was outweighed by its prejudicial effect (*R v Stewart* (1972));
   (b) where it was obtained by improper or unfair means;
   (c) where it was obtained in breach of Codes of Practice or the statutory provisions governing the detention and treatment of suspects.

4. The common law discretion remains useful in just one situation: where a judge admits a confession following a *voir dire*, but later changes his

view having heard the whole of the evidence, the common law power allows him to direct the jury to disregard the confession. Section 78(1) entitles a judge to exclude evidence 'on which the prosecution proposes to rely', and evidence cannot be retrospectively excluded once it has been adduced in open court.

10.5.2 Discretion under s78(1)

1. Section 78(1) states: 'In any proceedings the court may refuse to allow evidence on which the prosecution proposes to rely to be given if it appears to the court that, having regard to all the circumstances, including the circumstances in which the evidence was obtained, the admission of the evidence would have such an adverse effect on the fairness of the proceedings that the court ought not to admit it'.

2. This section extends to all prosecution evidence, not just confessions. It tends to be used quite commonly as a sanction against the police, although potentially it has a much wider use.

3. *R v Mason* (1987) remains the leading case on exclusion of confession evidence. The accused confessed to arson having been told by police officers that his fingerprints had been found at the scene. This was a lie designed to elicit a confession. The Court of Appeal held that the confession should have been excluded under s78(1).

4. Confession evidence may be excluded where a suspect detained for questioning at a police station is improperly denied access to legal advice.

5. The courts often look at the motives of the police officers in deciding whether or not to exercise discretion.
   (a) where they have acted in 'bad faith', a confession will be excluded; where they have acted in 'good faith' it may not.
   (b) In *R v Alladice* (1988) the Lord Chief Justice stated: 'If the police have acted in bad faith the court will have little difficulty in ruling any confession inadmissible under s78, if not under s76 ... If the police, albeit in good faith, have nevertheless fallen foul of s58, it is still necessary for the court to decide whether to admit the evidence would adversely affect the fairness of the proceedings, and would do so to such an extent that the confession ought to be excluded'.
   (c) But in *R v Samuel* (1988) it was made plain that this test will not be appropriate in all circumstances.

6. *R v Brine* (1992) illustrates that s78 is not concerned exclusively with misconduct by the police. The accused was suffering from a mild paranoid psychosis which would have made him feel threatened by questioning and prone to lie and falsely confess. There had been nothing said or done by the police which would render the confession unreliable under s76(2)(b), but the Court of Appeal held that s78 should have been used to exclude the confession on the grounds of fairness.

7. In *R v Quinn* (1990), it was explained that the function of the judge is to protect the fairness of the proceedings, and normally proceedings will be fair if a jury hears all relevant evidence which either side wishes to place before it, but proceedings may become unfair if, for example:
   - one side is allowed to adduce relevant evidence which, for one reason or another, the other side cannot properly challenge or meet; or
   - where there has been an abuse of process, e.g. because evidence has been obtained in deliberate breach of procedures laid down in an official code of practice.

8. In the absence of any misdirection by the trial judge, the Court of Appeal will be reluctant to interfere with the exercise of discretion.

10.6 Confessions by the mentally handicapped

1. Mental handicap is relevant both to admissibility under s76(2) and to discretion to exclude a confession either at common law or under s78(1).

2. Whilst Code C provides pre-trial protection by requiring the presence of an 'appropriate adult' at any interview with a mentally disordered person, s77(1) provides additional protection at trial.

3. Section 77(1) imposes a statutory responsibility on judges to warn a jury of the need for caution before relying upon a confession by a mentally handicapped person where the court is satisfied that:
   - he is mentally handicapped; and
   - the confession was not made in the presence of an independent person.

4. It is for the defence to establish on a balance of probabilities that the circumstances set out in s77(1) apply.

5. Section 77(3) defines mental handicap as 'a state of arrested or incomplete development of mind which includes significant impairment of intelligence and social functioning'.

6. Lord Taylor CJ provided further guidance to judges dealing with confessions by the mentally handicapped in the case of *R v McKenzie* (1993) where:
   (i) the prosecution case depends wholly upon confessions; and
   (ii) the accused suffers from a significant degree of mental handicap; and
   (iii) the confessions are unconvincing to a point where a jury properly directed could not properly convict upon them, then the judge, assuming he has not excluded the confessions earlier, should withdraw the case from the jury.

10.7 Facts discovered as a result of an inadmissible confession

1. At common law, incriminating facts discovered as a result of an inadmissible confession were admissible (*R v Warwickshall* (1783)).

2. The common law rule was given statutory force and clarification under s76(4) and (5) of PACE.

3. Evidence that a fact was discovered as a result of an inadmissible confession made by the accused cannot be led by the prosecution, but remains admissible if led by the accused or his counsel (s76(4)(a) and (5)). So, evidence discovered as a result of the inadmissible confession is admissible. The prosecution just can't tell the jury how they discovered it unless the defence do!

4. Under s76(4)(b), where something in an inadmissible confession shows that the accused speaks, writes or expresses himself in a particular manner, and this serves to identify him as the offender, that part of the confession is admissible as non-hearsay evidence: the purpose of admitting it is not to prove the truth of the words, simply to show the manner of writing or speaking.

5. Section 76(4) and (5) apply to confessions which are inadmissible under s76.

6. If a confession is excluded under s78, then the common law rules apply (*R v Warwickshall* (1783)).

11

Evidence obtained by illegal or unfair means

> **General rule:** evidence is admissible even where it is obtained illegally or unfairly, but may be excluded under the exercise of judicial discretion.

Exclusion at common law
- where probative value is outweighed by prejudicial effect;
- confession evidence;
- evidence obtained from accused after commission of offence.

Exclusion under s78 PACE
where the admission of evidence would have such an adverse effect on the fairness of the proceedings that it ought not to be admitted.

11.1 The general rule

1. There is no general rule excluding relevant evidence on the grounds that it was obtained illegally or improperly (for example, by means of a crime, trickery, deception or as a result of inducements). The only two exceptions to that rule relate to:
   - privileged documents (see 13.5); and
   - confessions (see 10.4).
2. The clearest statement of the common law position was delivered by Crompton J in *R v Leatham* (1861):

3. 'It matters not how you get it; if you steal it even, it would be admissible in evidence'.

4. In *Kuruma v R* (1955), where evidence was discovered in the course of an illegal search, it remained admissible, despite the fact that the search produced evidence of a capital offence.

5. At the other end of the spectrum, in *Jeffrey v Black* (1978) the defendant was suspected of stealing a sandwich. An illegal search of his home revealed a quantity of cannabis and he was charged with possession. The Court of Appeal held that the Magistrates' Court had erroneously excluded that evidence.

11.2 Discretion to exclude at common law

1. Section 82(3) of PACE 1984 retains the common law discretion to exclude admissible evidence, although its scope remains unclear, despite a House of Lords ruling in *R v Sang* (1980), which attempted to lay down guidelines.
   (a) Lord Diplock explained the general rule and the role of the judge to ensure fairness, but that 'What the judge at the trial is concerned with is not how the evidence sought to be adduced by the prosecution has been obtained, but with how it is used by the prosecution at trial'.
   (b) Viscount Dilhorne outlined the purpose of the common law discretion to exclude evidence by saying: 'It is not the manner in which [the evidence] has been obtained but its use at the trial if accompanied by prejudicial effects outweighing its probative value and so rendering the trial unfair to the accused which will justify the exercise of judicial discretion to exclude it'.
   (c) More confusingly, Lord Diplock emphasised that although a trial judge has discretion to exclude evidence where its prejudicial effect outweighs its probative value, the only common law discretion to exclude evidence relates to confession evidence, 'and … evidence obtained from the accused after commission of the offence'.

2. In *R v Sang*, Lord Diplock did acknowledge a limited discretionary power to exclude evidence owing to the way in which it was obtained rather than the way it was to be used at trial, for example where 'trickery' or other unfair means had been employed.

3. Few people claim to fully understand the ambit of the discretion as explained by the House of Lords in *R v Sang*, however, since the

enactment of PACE, the common law discretion has become virtually
redundant, with little, if any, distinction remaining between the two.

11.3 Discretion to exclude under s78(1) PACE 1984

1. Section 78(l) states: 'In any proceedings the court may refuse to allow
   evidence on which the prosecution proposes to rely to be given if
   it appears to the court that, having regard to all the circumstances,
   including the circumstances in which the evidence was obtained, the
   admission of the evidence would have such an adverse effect on the
   fairness of the proceedings that the court ought not to admit it'.

2. To date the power has not been used rigorously as a judicial tool to
   strengthen individual rights or maintain standards of propriety.

3. It is possible that s78(1) will be used more widely in the future in light
   of the new responsibilities imposed upon judges under s6 HRA 1998,
   although the evidence to date is not suggestive of a more proactive use.

4. As was considered above at 10.5.2, some judges appear to operate a
   good faith/bad faith test, using s78(1) to exclude evidence obtained
   illegally and in bad faith. This approach is illustrated by the cases of
   Matto v Crown Court at Wolverhampton (1987) and *Fox v Chief Constable
   of Gwent* (1986). Both cases involved the unlawful administration of a
   breath test to drivers suspected of driving with excess alcohol.
   (a) In *Matto*, the officers knew they were acting unlawfully, and the
       Court of Appeal held that the evidence relating to the test should
       have been excluded under s78(1).
   (b) Conversely, in *Fox*, officers believed, erroneously, that they were
       acting within the law. The Court of Appeal held that the evidence
       had been properly admitted.

5. The case of *R v Khan* (1997), which was considered by the Court of
   Appeal, the House of Lords and the European Court of Human Rights
   is regarded by many as disappointing in its failure to expand the use
   of s78(1) to strengthen human rights. Evidence was obtained by police
   officers using an unlawful surveillance technique, in contravention
   of Article 8 of the European Convention – the right to privacy. It was
   conceded by the prosecution that, in the absence of any lawful authori-
   sation, this form of covert surveillance amounted to a civil trespass.
   Nevertheless, all three courts found that the evidence obtained as a result
   of this unlawful operation was properly admitted at Khan's trial.

11.4 Entrapment

1. Entrapment means enticement to commit an offence that would not have been committed in the absence of enticement.

2. Undercover operations by police officers who have infiltrated criminal gangs in an attempt to gather information and evidence do not amount to entrapment.

3. The courts will not generally be prepared to exercise discretion under s78(1) to exclude evidence obtained in the course of undercover operations but they may be prepared to do so where an offence is procured by means of entrapment.

   - In *R v Christou* (1992), where police set up a jewellery shop visited by the defendant in an attempt to sell stolen jewellery, tape recordings of incriminatory conversations were not excluded by the court, since the defendant had not been tricked into committing an offence.
   - In *R v Smurthwaite* (1994) the defendant had sought to arrange the murder of his wife through an undercover police officer posing as a contract killer. Tape recordings of the conversations were properly admitted at trial since the operation involved no entrapment.

4. Guidance from the European Court of Human Rights was provided in the case of *Texeira de Castro v Portugal* (1999) where it was said: 'The general requirements of fairness embodied in Article 6 apply to proceedings concerning all types of criminal offence, from the most straightforward to the most complex. The public interest cannot justify the use of evidence obtained as a result of police incitement'.

5. Merely giving a defendant an opportunity to break the law is not entrapment (*Nottingham City Council v Amin* (2001)).

6. In *R v Loosely: Attorney General's Reference (No. 3 of 2000)* (2001), the House of Lords indicated that future cases will be decided on the basis of the abuse of process doctrine, rather than s78(1), on the basis that citizens shouldn't be lured into committing criminal activity then prosecuted for it. The effect of a successful abuse of process application would be the collapse of the prosecution case.

7. Applying the new 'abuse of process' approach to the cases discussed above, it is unlikely that a different decision would be reached. However in *R v Shannon* (2001), where there was clear evidence that the defendant was persuaded or pressurised into committing the offence, the Court of Appeal did consider applying the abuse of process doctrine.

Similarly, in *R v Moon* (2004) where the appellant, after considerable persuasion from an undercover police officer, had supplied a small quantity of heroin that she obtained from a supplier, the Court of Appeal held that the proceedings should have been stayed as an abuse of process. The appellant had been entrapped into committing a crime, and had made it clear to the officer that she would not be prepared to do so again.

In *R v Jones (Ian)* (2007) the appellant J was convicted of attempting to commit an offence under s8 of the Sexual Offences Act 2003. J had been responsible for graffiti in public toilets which invited girls aged between 8 and 13 to engage in sexual activity in return for payment. A journalist contacted the police after seeing the graffiti, and the police used an undercover officer, posing as a twelve year-old girl, to set up a meeting at which the appellant was arrested. The Court of Appeal looked closely at the nature and extent of the police's participation in the crime. It was held there was no 'ulterior motive other than to apprehend the appellant and to provide the necessary evidence'. There was a clear record of what the officer had done and it was not a case involving a vulnerable defendant. The police's actions were proportionate and did not contravene Article 8 of the ECHR.

12

Opinion evidence

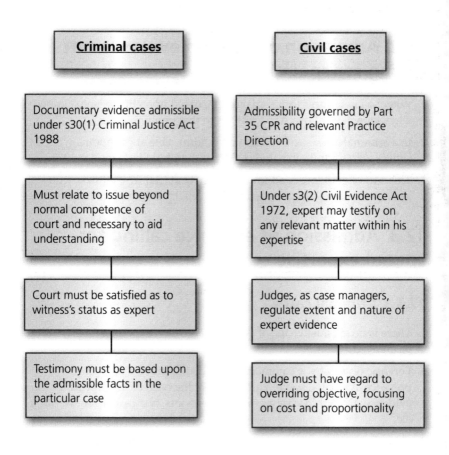

Criminal cases

Documentary evidence admissible under s30(1) Criminal Justice Act 1988

Must relate to issue beyond normal competence of court and necessary to aid understanding

Court must be satisfied as to witness's status as expert

Testimony must be based upon the admissible facts in the particular case

Civil cases

Admissibility governed by Part 35 CPR and relevant Practice Direction

Under s3(2) Civil Evidence Act 1972, expert may testify on any relevant matter within his expertise

Judges, as case managers, regulate extent and nature of expert evidence

Judge must have regard to overriding objective, focusing on cost and proportionality

12.1 Introduction

1. The general rule is that opinion evidence is inadmissible in both criminal and civil cases: witnesses can testify only as to matters of fact within their own personal knowledge.

2. Exceptions to this rule are:
   (a) witnesses are allowed to give statements of opinion based on their own personal knowledge and not calling for special expertise;
   (b) witnesses who satisfy the court of their 'expert' status are allowed to give opinion evidence within their field of expertise;
   (c) in civil cases, opinion evidence relating to matters of public concern and family history is admissible.

12.2 Admission of opinion evidence not calling for special expertise

1. Where a lay witness forms an opinion, based upon his personal knowledge, he will be allowed to testify as to that opinion.

2. In a criminal case, such a statement is admissible at common law; in a civil case it is admissible under s3(2) of the Civil Evidence Act 1972.

3. This sort of evidence is admitted routinely at trial: any witness who gives evidence relating to identity is, in effect, giving opinion evidence.

12.3 Admission of evidence calling for special expertise

12.3.1 Criminal cases

1. There is no exhaustive list of issues upon which expert testimony will be allowed.

2. Forensic testimony is commonly admitted to prove a defendant's presence at a crime scene. This may take the form of fingerprint evidence, DNA, bloodstains, fibres, footprints, tyre prints, handwriting, etc.

3. Other issues on which expert testimony has been allowed include:
   - psychological evidence when considering a defence of diminished responsibility or insanity (*R v Ahluwalia* (1992));
   - psychological effects on children of 'battle cards', given away free with chewing gum (*DPP v ABC Chewing Gum* (1968));
   - changes to the stock market;
   - earprints;

- foreign law;
- artistic merit;
- facial mapping;
- voice identification; and virtually any other issue outside the ordinary competence of the court.

4. A written report from an expert witness is admissible under s30(1) of the Criminal Justice Act 1988, whether or not the expert is called to testify in person.

5. Admissibility depends upon two factors:

   (a) **It must relate to an issue that goes beyond the normal competence of the court and must be necessary to aid the court in understanding the issue or reaching a decision on the facts.**

   - In *R v Land* (1999), L was convicted of possessing indecent photographs of a child. The trial judge directed the jury they should use their own judgement, experience and critical faculties to decide the age of the children in the photographs. L appealed on the basis that a paediatrician should have performed this function. The Court of Appeal held that the jury was as well placed as an expert to make this decision.

   - *R v Turner* (1975) establishes that expert evidence is inadmissible:
     - when it concerns an issue within the knowledge of the jury; and
     - when it concerns an issue of human nature and behaviour within the bounds of normality.

   - The Court of Appeal rejected the use of expert evidence to show the *mens rea* of the accused and to shed light on his credibility. T wished to use a psychiatrist to support a partial defence of provocation under s3 of the Homicide Act 1957. T had killed his girlfriend after flying into a rage when she confessed to numerous instances of infidelity and that she was pregnant with another man's child. T wished to call expert evidence to confirm that, although not suffering from any mental illness, he was of a personality to be severely provoked by his girlfriend's disclosure. Lawton LJ stated: 'jurors do not need psychiatrists to tell them how ordinary folk who are not suffering from any mental illness are likely to react to the stresses and strains of life' and the expert evidence was inadmissible.

- Where a defence of diminished responsibility under s2 of the Homicide Act 1957 is raised, expert evidence will invariably be admitted because the court or jury is unlikely to have sufficient knowledge of mental abnormality to reach a safe conclusion without help (*R v Dix* (1982)).
- Where a defendant relies on a defence of non-insane automatism, this will be outside the knowledge of the jury, even though it does not amount to a mental illness (*R v Smith* (1979)).
- Where a defendant is intellectually impaired but is considered 'normal', with an IQ of 70 or above, the courts have ruled expert evidence as to the impairment is inadmissible at trial (*R v Masih* (1986). This rule appears to have been relaxed where a court's considers the admissibility of confession evidence under s76 PACE 1984 at a *voir dire* hearing (*R v Silcott*, (1991)).
- The courts have extended recognised mental illnesses to cover post-traumatic stress disorders (*R v White* (1995) and *R v Huckerby* (2004)).

(b) **Before expert evidence can be admitted at trial, the court must be satisfied as to the witness's status as an expert and this will involve a consideration of his qualifications and experience.**

- The burden of proof in establishing expertise lies with the party seeking to call the witness. In *R v Silverlock* (1894), a solicitor who studied handwriting in his spare time, was able to give evidence as an expert witness. This case illustrates that expertise need not be attained in the course of a profession and an 'expert' need not possess formal qualifications. Only forensic scientists must possess a formal qualification.
- Where there are concerns regarding the quality of an expert's evidence the courty can refuse to admit it (*R v Inch* (1990) but an expert who produces contentious evidence or that which conflicts with others in his field may not necessarily be refused (*R v Robb* (1991)).
- An expert must confine his evidence to his specific area of expertise *R v Barnes* (2005).

6. The weight that is attributed to expert evidence is generally a matter for the jury and the standard Judicial Studies Board direction reflects this. Where a jury rejects very strong and undisputed evidence given by an expert, this may lead to the conviction being quashed (see *R v Smith* (1999)).

7. Historically, the admission of an expert's opinion evidence, based upon the views of other people, has presented problems under the hearsay rule in criminal cases. This has been partially solved by Part 33 Criminal Procedure Rules 2010 and by ss114(1)(b) and 127 CJA 2003. Section 114(1)(b) preserves expert reports as evidence of facts stated therein and where such evidence is admitted, 'the statement is to be treated as evidence of what it states' (s127(3)). The court retains power to order that the statement is not so used in the interests of justice (s127(4)). The court will consider the practicality, cost and effectiveness of calling the person or persons upon which the expert's evidence was based.

8. Procedural matters regarding expert evidence can be found in Part 33 of the Criminal Procedure Rules 2010.

12.3.2 Civil cases

1. In civil cases, the nature of admissible expert evidence is just as varied as in criminal cases.

2. Admissibility is governed by Part 35 of the Civil Procedure Rules (CPR 35) and the relevant Practice Direction to Part 35.

3. In an attempt to eradicate the pre-Woolf 'battle of the experts' problems associated with expert testimony, judges have assumed responsibility for regulating the extent and nature of expert evidence under their new role as Case Managers.

4. Expert witnesses today owe an overriding duty to the court, not to the party who calls and pays them.

5. On the small claims track, expert evidence will rarely be admissible; on the fast track, such evidence may be restricted to the admission of written reports; on the multi-track, the judge may rule that one agreed expert be called instead of each party calling its own witness. Where the parties cannot agree upon a common expert, the court has power to appoint an expert of its choosing.

6. A judge must have regard to the overriding objective to deal with each case justly, and this requires him to focus on cost and proportionality, bearing in mind the value of the claim.

7. Section 3(2) of the Civil Evidence Act 1972 governs the nature of admissible expert evidence:

'where a person is called as a witness in civil proceedings, his opinion on any relevant matter on which he is qualified to give expert evidence, shall be admissible'.

8. CPR 35 states: 'Expert evidence should be restricted to that which is reasonably required to resolve the proceedings'.

12.4 Opinion evidence on matters of public concern and family history

1. A third exception allowing for the admission of non-expert opinion evidence exists by virtue of a common law rule, which was preserved by s7(3) of the Civil Evidence Act 1995. This allows for evidence relating to such matters as family history, reputation, or the existence of a marriage.

2. The weight accorded to such evidence will be a matter for the court to decide.

12.5 Testifying as to the ultimate issue

1. At common law, experts were not entitled to give evidence as to the ultimate issue, i.e. the defendant's guilt or innocence. Witnesses were required to circumvent the rule by choosing their words carefully.

2. The case of *R v Stockwell* (1995) effectively witnessed the final demise of this rule, when an expert in facial mapping testified that, based on the measurements he had taken from the security video and the defendant's face, there was strong evidence to suggest that the defendant was the person depicted on the videotape. It is generally recognised today that this rule has little relevance.

3. The modern position is that an expert can testify as to the ultimate issue providing the jury is directed that they are not required to accept the opinion of the expert on that matter.

4. In *R v Till* (2005) the Court of Appeal upheld the decision of the trial judge to refuse to admit evidence from an expert supporting the appellant's contention that his driving was careless but not dangerous. It was held that the judge was right to leave the ultimate issue to the jury, unhampered by conclusions drawn from expert opinion.

5. In civil cases, the ultimate issue will involve the question of liability. Whilst historically, experts were not permitted to testify as to the ultimate issue in civil cases, s3(1) of the Civil Evidence Act 1972 does provide for the admission of opinion evidence 'on any relevant matter'. The ultimate issue is arguably the most relevant issue before the court, hence it is generally accepted that s3(1) has supplanted the common law rule. The court today is free to accord whatever weight it feels appropriate to the evidence of an expert witness on the ultimate issue.

13

Privilege, public policy and disclosure

APPLIES	COVERS	
Privilege against self-incrimination	Witnesses	Refusal to answer questions
Legal-professional privilege	Clients of solicitors	Communications between solicitor and client; communications between solicitor and third party where dominant purpose relates to litigation
Without prejudice negotiations	Parties to litigation	Statements made without prejudice during discussions/correspondence aimed at avoiding litigation

13.1 Introduction to privilege

There are three types of privilege that may give rise to the exclusion of relevant evidence:

- the privilege against self-incrimination;
- legal professional privilege; and
- 'without prejudice' negotiations.

13.2 The privilege against self-incrimination

1. The privilege against self-incrimination applies in both criminal and civil proceedings and entitles witnesses to refuse to answer questions or to produce relevant documents in circumstances where such evidence might give rise to a criminal charge or criminal sanction. Note the privilege does not extend to the risk of proceedings being brought in foreign jurisdictions.

2. The privilege belongs to the witness and must be claimed by that witness during the course of testimony.

3. Where the privilege is not claimed, incriminatory answers remain admissible and may be used in criminal proceedings against the witness.

4. The ambit of the rule was explained in *Blunt v Park Lane Hotel* (1942): 'The rule is that no-one is bound to answer any question if the answer thereto would, in the opinion of the judge, have a tendency to expose [him] to any criminal charge or penalty which the judge regards as reasonably likely to be preferred or sued for'.

5. A witness may refuse to answer questions that might incriminate his/her spouse or civil partner. This privilege is recognised in criminal proceedings and has statutory force in civil proceedings under s14(1)(b) Civil Evidence Act 1968. It should be noted that the privilege is that of the witness, not the spouse or civil partner and if the witness chooses to answer questions of an incriminatory nature, s/he is entitled to do so.

6. The scope of the privilege against incrimination is partially restricted by the following statutes:
   (a) Section 31(1) of the Theft Act 1968 provides that a witness may not refuse to answer questions in proceedings for the recovery of property or the execution of a trust on the grounds that his answer might lay him open to a charge under the Act.
   (b) Section 2 of the Criminal Justice Act 1987 allows the Serious Fraud Squad to compel a person to answer questions in the context of a serious fraud inquiry.
   (c) Section 98 of the Children Act 1989 provides that a witness must answer questions in proceedings related to the care, supervision or protection of a child.
   (d) Section 72 of the Supreme Court Act 1981 prevents the privilege being used in civil disputes in the area of intellectual property.

Under these statutes, the restriction to the privilege is partial, since answers obtained by compulsion are not admissible in subsequent criminal proceedings.

7. By virtue of a number of other statutes, including the Companies Act 1985, such answers were admissible in subsequent criminal proceedings.

13.3 Self-incrimination and human rights

1. In *Saunders v UK* (1997) the ECtHR found there was a breach of Article 6 and stressed that the right not to incriminate oneself lay at the heart of the concept of a fair trial within Article 6.

2. As a result of the *Saunders* decision in the ECtHR, s59 and Schedule 3 YJCEA 1999 amended s434 of the Companies Act 1985 and a number of other statutes that purported to admit answers compelled during a non-judicial investigation.

3. A number of statutes, including the Road Traffic Act 1988 (RTA 1988) and legislation in the area of environmental protection (see *R v Hertfordshire CC ex p Green Environmental Industries* (2000)), require information to be provided that might be of a self-incriminatory nature. These statutes are generally designed to tackle serious social problems and are not covered by s59 YJCEA 1999.

4. The present situation seems to be that where the prosecution seeks to rely upon answers obtained from defendants under compulsion at a subsequent criminal trial, judges are obliged to consider the fair trial requirements of Article 6(1), using s78 of PACE 1984 to exclude evidence where its admission would adversely affect the fairness of the trial.

5. The Privy Council in *Brown v Stott* (2001) considered s172(a) RTA 1988 which requires the registered keeper of a vehicle to provide details of the driver when investigating offences under the Act, for example, driving with excess alcohol. The Privy Council had to decide whether interference with the privilege against self-incrimination was a proportionate response to the problem of road safety and vehicle misuse. They concluded that it was and this decision was clarified by the Grand Chamber of the ECtHR in two RTA 1988 cases: *Francis v UK* (2007) and *O'Halloran v UK* (2007). In deciding that the interference with the privilege against self-incrimination was

proportionate, Grand Chamber used a test created in the case of *Jalloh v Germany* (2007). The Court must have regard to:

- the nature and degree of compulsion used to obtain the evidence;
- the weight of the public interest in the investigation and punishment of the offence at issue;
- the existence of any relevant safeguards in the procedure; and
- the use to which any material so obtained is put.

13.4 Legal professional privilege

1. Legal professional privilege enables confidentiality to be maintained in two types of situation:
   (a) communications between a client and lawyer made for the purpose of obtaining and giving legal advice; and
   (b) communications between a client or his lawyer and third parties (such as potential witnesses and experts) brought into existence in contemplation of a criminal trial or litigation.

2. The rationale behind the privilege was expressed by Lord Taylor CJ in *R v Derby Magistrates' Court, ex parte B* (1996): 'The principle that runs through [the law] … is that a man must be able to consult his lawyer in confidence, since otherwise he might hold back half the truth. The client must be sure that what he tells the lawyer in confidence will never be revealed without his consent. Legal professional privilege is thus much more than an ordinary rule of evidence, limited in its application to the facts of a particular case. It is a fundamental condition on which the administration of justice as a whole rests'.

3. A justification for legal professional privilege was given by Lord Scott of Foscote in the important House of Lords decision, *Three Rivers DC v Governor and Company of the Bank of England (No 6)* (2004):'[It] is necessary in … a society in which the restraining and controlling framework is built upon a belief in the rule of law that communications between clients and lawyers, whereby the clients are hoping for the assistance of the lawyers' legal skills in the management of their … affairs, should be secure against the possibility of any scrutiny from others, whether the police, the executive, business competitors, inquisitive busy-bodies or anyone else … It justifies, in my opinion, the retention of legal advice privilege in our law, notwithstanding that as a result cases may sometimes have to be decided in ignorance of relevant probative material'.

4. To qualify for privileged status,
   (a) communications between client and lawyer must have been confidential in nature, and
   (b) if not actually made in the course of a lawyer/client relationship, must have been made with a view to establishing such a relationship.

5. The privilege extends to instructions by the client to his solicitor and from solicitor to barrister. Traditionally, it was believed to extend also to communications between lawyer or client and third parties, providing the dominant purpose of the communication was to obtain legal advice in connection with litigation or to collect evidence for use in litigation.

6. In *Waugh v British Railways Board* (1980) the House of Lords held that in order for communications with third parties to attract privilege, the dominant purpose for the preparation of the reports must have been for submission to a legal advisor for use in litigation.

7. The rule was restricted by the Court of Appeal in *Three Rivers DC v Governor and Company of the Bank of England (No 5)* (2003): before documents sent to legal advisers can attract privilege, litigation must genuinely be in prospect or the court must be satisfied that the communication is for the purpose of taking legal advice. Lord Scott, on appeal to the House of Lords, added that there must be a 'relevant legal context' before advice can attract privilege.

8. A pre-existing document given into the custody of a solicitor for the purpose of obtaining such advice, or sent to a third party in connection with litigation, is no more privileged than if it remained with the client (*R v Peterborough Justices, ex parte Hicks* (1977); *R v King* (1983)).

9. The House of Lords confirmed in *Derby Magistrates' Court, ex parte B* (1996) that legal professional privilege between a client and his legal advisers is absolute. The appellant, B, sought judicial review of the magistrates' decision to issue witness summonses to him and his solicitor requiring attendance notes and proofs of evidence in respect of his defence to a murder charge. B had initially told the police that he was responsible for the murder of a 16-year- old girl. He later withdrew the statement, blaming his stepfather for the murder and was acquitted. The appellant's stepfather argued that the public interest in securing all relevant evidence for the defence outweighed the need to protect the solicitor and client relationship. The House of Lords upheld the privilege and in doing so, overruled the previous decisions in *R v Barton* (1973) and *R v Ataou* (1988).

13.4.1 Exceptions to the privilege

Privilege can be lost in the following ways:

1. **Where advice is sought in furtherance of fraud or some other criminal purpose**.

   (a) The common law rule is illustrated by the old case of *R v Cox & Railton* (1884) and was given statutory force under s10(2) PACE 1984, which provides that 'items held with the intention of furthering a criminal purpose are not items subject to legal privilege'.

   (b) The case of *Francis & Francis v Central Criminal Court* (1988) confirmed that s10(2) was not meant to restrict the common law rule, merely to reinforce it.

2. **Where secondary evidence is obtained by another party.**

   (a) Privilege attaches to conversations between solicitors and clients as well as to documents brought into existence in contemplation of litigation. It attaches to the original document and to copies made for the purpose of instructing a lawyer.

   (b) If a document, or a copy of it falls into the wrong hands, or a privileged conversation is overheard, then the privilege may be lost.

   (c) In *R v Tompkins* (1977), an incriminating note from the accused to his counsel was found on the floor of the court and handed to prosecuting counsel. The Court of Appeal upheld the judge's ruling that the prosecution could cross-examine the accused on the matters referred to in the note.

   ■ Where a copy of a privileged document comes into the possession of another party, that party may use the document as secondary evidence.

   ■ The party to whom the privilege attaches may, where the error is discovered at an early stage, seek a court order for the copies to be delivered up and an injunction to restrain the other party from disclosing or making use of the information contained in the document (*Guinness Peat Properties Ltd v Fitzroy Robinson Partnership* (1987)).

   ■ *Lord Ashburton v Pape* (1913) illustrates that where copies of privileged correspondence are obtained by means of a trick, the court will be more than willing to grant an injunction.

3. **Where privilege is waived.**

   (a) The party entitled to claim it can always waive privilege, but once waived, it cannot then be reasserted in relation to that communication/document.

   (b) If part of a privileged document is put in evidence, the other party can require the whole document to be disclosed, so waiver of part of a document loses privilege in respect of the entire contents.

   (c) Where a defendant exercises his right to silence on the advice of his solicitor, but waives privilege in order to avoid adverse inferences being drawn under s34 CJPOA 1994, the extent to which disclosure will be permitted is subject to a test of 'fairness' (*R v Loizou* (2006)). (see 6.2.9 above).

13.5 Without prejudice negotiations

1. Communications between opposing parties to litigation or their solicitors do not normally attract legal professional privilege. Because of that risk, privilege does attach to statements made **without prejudice**, i.e. without prejudice to the maker if the terms he proposes are not accepted.

2. If negotiations succeed and a settlement is reached, the without prejudice correspondence remains privileged.

3. Such correspondence is inadmissible in subsequent litigation on the same subject matter, whether between the same or different parties. One of the major aims of the Civil Procedure Rules was to actively encourage negotiation between disputing parties in an attempt to produce early settlements and avoid litigation.

4. The privilege is the joint privilege of both parties, and extends to their solicitors. It can only be waived with the consent of both parties.

5. The privilege attaches to any discussions or correspondence between actual or prospective parties with a view to avoiding litigation, even where the term 'without prejudice' is not expressly used (*Rush & Tompkins v Greater London Council* (1989)).

13.5.1 Exceptions

1. Without prejudice material is admissible if the issue between the parties at trial is whether or not the negotiations resulted in an agreed settlement.

2. Each party may agree that a without prejudice document should be disclosed to the court.

3. Without prejudice negotiations may be disclosed where they have been used as a vehicle for fraud.

4. Without prejudice correspondence may be entered into with the express limitation that if a settlement is not reached, the correspondence can be referred to the judge on the issue of costs.

13.6 Exclusion of evidence on the ground of public policy (public interest immunity)

Despite the general rule that all relevant evidence is admissible and subject to the rules on disclosure, a direct conflict may sometimes arise between the interests of the state in non-disclosure and the interests of justice and those of the defendant or party to a civil action in disclosing all relevant evidence.

1. A successful application for the exclusion of evidence on the grounds of public interest immunity (PII) will prevent the disclosure of information on the basis that it would be detrimental to the 'public good'. The main 'heads' of public interest put forward in PII applications relate to:

- documents concerning national security or high-level affairs of the state;
- national and local governmental policy documents;
- documents relating to the prevention and detection of crime; and
- documents that are confidential.

2. PII is most commonly claimed by civil servants or the police but can also be claimed by other bodies for example, the NSPCC (see *D v NSPCC* (1978); *Rogers v Home Secretary* (1973); *R v Reading Justices ex parte Berkshire County Council* (1996); and *R v Brushett* (2001)).

13.6.1 Public interest immunity in civil cases

1. In civil cases, the procedure for claiming PII is governed by Rule 31.19 of the Civil Procedure Rules 1998. Rule 31.19 makes clear it is open to *any* person to apply to the court for an order withholding information on the basis of PII. The order can be made *ex parte* and may not only prevent inspection of a document by the other side but also its disclosure and discovery. In certain extreme cases, the other party may not be aware of the PII application having been made. (For the Human Rights implications of such applications see 13.7 below.).

2. Traditionally, PII was claimed either because the nature of a specific document is sensitive (a contents claim) or because a document falls into a class of documents, the whole class of which should be excluded in the public interest (a class claim).

3. Historically, the courts adopted the notion that a mere claim of public interest immunity by a minister in respect of any document was conclusive (*Duncan v Cammell Laird & Co Ltd* (1942)).

4. A different approach to that in *Duncan v Cammell Laird & Co Ltd* (1942) was adopted in *Conway v Rimmer* (1968), which was historic for two reasons:
   (i) it was the first case in which the House of Lords made use of Lord Gardiner's Practice Statement of 1966 by departing from a previous House of Lords decision;
   (ii) it was the first occasion that a claim of public interest immunity by a minister was not upheld. Their Lordships held that it was for the trial judge, not the minister, to decide whether or not to order disclosure where a claim of public interest immunity was made.

5. In *Conway v Rimmer* Lord Reid acknowledged that certain classes of document, such as cabinet papers, ought never to be disclosed unless of historical interest only. However, in *Burmah Oil v Bank of England* (1979), the House of Lords expressed the view that even the 'most sensitive documents at the highest level' may require inspection by the judge and in *Air Canada v Secretary of State for Trade and Industry* (1983) it was made clear that even the minutes of cabinet meetings were not immune. Following the publication of the Scott Report in 1996, government ministers are no longer able to claim PII in respect of class claims. The House of Lords looked at this in the case of *R v Chief Constable of the West Midlands ex parte Wiley* (1995), suggesting that persons or bodies holding sensitive information should conduct an

initial balancing exercise to determine whether disclosure was possible despite the sensitive nature of the documents. Where a PII claim is based on national security, however, the courts generally take the view that the minister in question is best placed to make a decision and the courts will rarely object (*Balfour v Foreign Office* (1994)).

6. In civil cases judges must perform a balancing exercise between the competing interests.
   (a) On the one hand is the public interest in the administration of justice that requires all relevant evidence to be disclosed at trial.
   (b) Weighed against that important interest is the need to protect sensitive information that might be damaging either to national security or individuals.

7. The trial judge must keep his decision under review throughout the proceedings and if the result of the balancing exercise changes, it may be necessary to order disclosure. Often the effect of such a decision will mean the party claiming PII discontinues the action (see *R v Davis* (1993)).

13.6.2 Public interest immunity in criminal cases

1. In criminal cases, claims for the exclusion of evidence on the ground of PII are recognised under s21(2) CPIA 1996 (as amended by CJA 2003). The Act requires full prosecution disclosure subject to the common law rules on PII. The procedures for claiming PII are set out in Part 22 of the Criminal Procedure Rules 2010.

2. In *R v Governor of Pentonville Prison, ex parte Osman (No1)* (1992) it was acknowledged that the law on PII established by the civil courts also applied in principle in the criminal courts but it was emphasised that a different balancing exercise is required in criminal cases: the weight to be attached to the interests of justice in disclosing all relevant evidence in a criminal case touching upon and concerning liberty, is very great indeed. This was not a new sentiment: indeed in *Marks v Beyfus* (1890) very similar view was expressed by Esher MR.

3. *Marks v Beyfus* concerned evidence furnished by a police informer, and this is an area where the scales will normally tip in favour of non-disclosure. The public interest in encouraging people to provide information on criminal activities is itself worthy of protection, thus the burden lies with the defence to show that disclosure of an informer's identity is necessary to the proper presentation of a defence at trial (*R v Hennessey* (1968)).

In *R v Johnson* (1988) a PII application was made in respect of the location of a police observation post. The Court of Appeal gave guidance that an officer of at least sergeant rank should visit the property being used to conduct observations and establish the views of the occupiers to disclosure. This should then be supported by a visit by an officer of at least chief inspector rank immediately before trial. The attitude of the occupiers to disclosure will inform the 'balancing exercise' conducted by the judge.

In *R v West* (2005), W appealed against his conviction for possessing Class A drugs with intent to supply. His house had been searched by police on the basis of information from an informer, the identity of whom was withheld on the grounds of public interest immunity. W claimed at trial that the drugs had been planted by his supplier and he had been framed and the trial judge told the jury that had information been available to support this defence it would have been disclosed. On appeal it was acknowledged by the Crown that such information was in fact available and W's conviction was quashed by the Court of Appeal.

Lord Taylor CJ in *R v Keane* (1994) emphasised that:
'If the disputed material may prove the accused's innocence or avoid a miscarriage of justice, then the balance comes down resoundingly in favour of disclosing it'. Care must be taken, however to ensure a defence has not been concocted to obtain the identity of an informer (*R v Turner* (1995)).

3.7 Public interest immunity and human rights

The position of the ECtHR in criminal cases is that the prosecution has a duty to disclose any evidence in their possession that might assist an accused in establishing his innocence or obtaining a reduction in sentence.

This stance was demonstrated by the Court in *Rowe v UK* (2000): 'It is a fundamental aspect of the right to a fair trial that criminal proceedings ... should be adversarial and that there should be equality of arms between the prosecution and defence. The right to an adversarial trial means, in a criminal case, that both prosecution and defence must be given the opportunity to have knowledge of and comment on the observations filed and the evidence adduced by the other party'.

3. Importantly, the Court did acknowledge in the same case, that it may sometimes be necessary 'to withhold certain evidence from the defence so as to preserve the fundamental rights of another individual or to safeguard an important public interest'.

4. Where information is withheld there must be procedures employed at trial which sufficiently counterbalance any prejudice to the accused. So where an application was made *ex parte* but the accused was given as much information as possible and permitted to make representations on his limited knowledge of the information (which ultimately did not form part of the prosecution case), there was no violation of Article 6 ECHR (*Jasper v United Kingdom* (2000)). Even where the Grand Chamber of the ECtHR has held that a defendant was denied the ability to participate in the adversarial process with 'equality of arms', the situation may be saved by the Court of Appeal's review of the case (*Edwards v UK* (1992)).

5. In *R v H* (2004) the House of Lords considered *ex parte* PII applications and the potential need to appoint 'special counsel' to ensure compliance with Article 6 ECHR. Lord Bingham reasserted the 'golden rule of full disclosure' and formulated a series of questions which should be addressed before derogating from it:
   1 What is the material which the prosecution wishes to withhold? The Court must give detailed consideration to this.
   2 Is the material such that it as may weaken the prosecution case or strengthen that of the defence? If it is not, the disclosure should not be ordered. If it is, full disclosure, subject to (3), (4) and (5) below, should be ordered.
   3 Is there a real risk of prejudice to an important public interest (and, if so, what) if full disclosure of the material is ordered? If not full disclosure should be ordered.
   4 If the answer to (2) and (3) is *yes*, can the defendant's interest be protected without disclosure or disclosure be ordered to an extent or in a way which will give adequate protection to the public interest in question and also afford adequate protection to the interests of the defence? This question requires the court to consider, with specific reference to the material which the prosecution seek to withhold and the facts of the case and the defence as disclosed, whether the prosecution should formally admit what the defence seek to establish or whether disclosure short of full disclosure may be ordered. This may be done in appropriate cases by the preparation of summaries or extracts of evidence, or the provision of documents

in an edited or anonymised form, provided the documents supplied are approved by the judge. In appropriate cases, the appointment of special counsel may be a necessary step to ensure that the contentions of the prosecution are tested and the interests of the defendant protected. ..... In cases of exceptional difficulty the court may require the appointment of special counsel to ensure a correct answer to questions (2),(3) and (4).

5 Do the measures proposed in answer to (4) represent the minimum derogation to protect the public interest in question? If notNo, the court should order such greater disclosure as will represent the minimum derogation from the golden rule of full disclosure.

6 If limited disclosure is ordered pursuant to (4) or (5), may the effect be to render the trial process, viewed as a whole, unfair to the defendant? If yes, then fuller disclosure should be ordered even if this leads or may lead the prosecution to discontinue the proceedings so as to avoid having to make disclosure.

7 If the answer to (6) when first given is *no*, does that remain the correct answer as the trial unfolds, evidence is adduced and the defence advanced? It is important that the answer to (6) should not be treated as a final, once-and-for-all, answer but as a provisional answer which the courts must keep under review.

13.8 Disclosure

■ Rules on disclosure are different in criminal and civil cases. In criminal cases the most important disclosure rules are provided by the Criminal Procedure and Investigations Act 1996 (CPIA 1996), as amended by CJA 2003. In civil proceedings on the fast track and multi-track, disclosure is governed by Part 31 Civil Procedure Rules.

■ The purpose of disclosure is explained in the Attorney-General's Guidelines, published in April 2005:
'The scheme set out in the Criminal Procedure and Investigations Act 1996 (as amended by the CJA 2003) (the Act) is designed to ensure that there is fair disclosure of material which may be relevant to an investigation and which does not form part of the prosecution case. Disclosure under the Act should assist the accused in the timely preparation and presentation of their case and assist the court to focus on all the relevant issues in the trial. Disclosure which does not meet these objectives risks preventing a fair trial taking place'.

13.8.1 Disclosure requirement on the prosecution in crown court trials

1. The Code of Practice in Part II CPIA 1996 requires investigating officers to record relevant information, and to reveal to the prosecutor material that may be relevant to the investigation. Where there is any doubt about the relevance of material, the investigator should retain it.

2. Section 3 CPIA 1996, as amended by s32 CJA 2003, requires 'initial prosecution disclosure' of evidence which 'might reasonably be considered capable of undermining the case for the prosecution or of assisting the case for the accused.'. Where there is no such evidence, the prosecutor must provide the accused with a written statement to that effect. The Attorney General's Guidelines provide examples of such material:

   ■ any material casting doubt upon the accuracy of any prosecution evidence;
   ■ any material which may point to another person, whether charged or not (including a co-accused) having involvement in the commission of the offence;
   ■ any material which may cast doubt upon the reliability of a confession;
   ■ any material that might go to the credibility of a prosecution witness;
   ■ any material that might support a defence that is either raised by the defence or apparent from the prosecution papers;
   ■ any material which may have a bearing on the admissibility of any prosecution evidence.

13.8.2 Defence disclosure in crown court trials

1. Disclosure requirements on the defence have become much more rigorous since s6A CPIA 1996 (as amended by s32 CJA 2003) came into force in April 2005. The defence statement must be in writing and:

   ■ set out the nature of the defence, including any particular defence on which the accused intends to rely;
   ■ indicate the matters of fact on which he takes issue with the prosecution;
   ■ set out, in the case of each matter, why he takes issue with the prosecution; and
   ■ indicate any point of law that he wishes to take and any authority on which he intends to rely for that purpose.

Note there is no obligation on the defendant to disclose 'unused' material.

2. Section 6C CPIA 1996 (as amended by s34 CJA 2003 but not yet in force) requires defendants to indicate sufficient details to identify witnesses intended to be called at trial. This will enable the prosecution to conduct pre-trial interview with witnesses.

3. Section 6D CPIA 1996 (inserted by s35 CJA 2003 but not yet in force) requires the defence to disclose details of any expert witness approached for the purpose of compiling a report for possible use at trial.

13.8.3 Continuing duty of disclosure in crown court trials

1. Section 7A CPIA 1996 imposes a continuing duty on the prosecutor to 'keep under review the question whether at any given time (and in particular, following the giving of a defence statement) there is prosecution material which:
   (a) might reasonably be considered capable of undermining the case for the prosecution against the accused or of assisting the case for the accused; and
   (b) has not been disclosed to the accused.

13.8.4 Sanctions for non-disclosure in crown court trials

1. Sanctions on the prosecution for non-disclosure include the quashing of convictions on appeal (see *R v Patel and Others* (2001) and *R v Craven* (2001)), or a stay of proceedings for abuse of process.

2. Under s11 CPIA 1996 a jury may draw adverse inferences from a defendant's failure to comply with disclosure requirements. Inferences may be drawn for:
   - failure to serve an initial defence statement or serving it out of time;
   - failing to send an updated statement when required to do so or serving it out of time;
   - pleading inconsistent defences in the defence statement;
   - advancing a defence at trial which is different to any previously disclosed;
   - advancing a defence at trial that has not previously been disclosed;

- failure to give evidence of alibi or calling a witness to give evidence in support of alibi without complying with the provisions relating to notification of alibi witnesses; and
- calling a witness who was not identified in the defence statement or advance notice of witnesses section (not yet in force).

3. Both prosecutor and the judge will be entitled to make comment to the jury on a failure to disclose although the judge must direct the jury and inferences alone will be insufficient to found a conviction (s11(10)). Where it appears to a judge at a pre-trial hearing that inferences may be drawn he should warn the accused of this (s11(5)).

13.8.5 Disclosure regime in summary trials

1. The Attorney-General's Guidelines on Disclosure (2005) offers guidance in summary trials: 'The prosecutor should, in addition to complying with the obligations under the Act, provide to the defence all evidence upon which the Crown proposes to rely in a summary trial. Such provision should allow the accused and their legal advisers sufficient time properly to consider the evidence before it is called'.

2. Section 1(1) CPIA 1996 partially incorporates the statutory scheme into summary trials by imposing a duty on the prosecutor to disclose any unused material to the defence where the accused pleads not guilty and the case proceeds to summary trial.

3. At this stage, under s6, the defence may voluntarily serve a defence statement on the prosecutor and the court. This has the effect of exposing the accused to inferences and comment on any inadequacies in the statement and is therefore rarely taken up by the defence.

Index